BINGHAM'S CHILL

of the

TWENTIETH CENTURY

by

CATHERINE HAYNES & HILDA SMITH

'Memories for the Millennium'

by the

**Nottinghamshire Living History Archive
Millennium Award Scheme**

A MILLENNIUM AWARD SCHEME
SUPPORTED BY FUNDS
FROM THE NATIONAL LOTTERY

City of
NOTTINGHAM

First Edition

Published by the 'Nottinghamshire Living History Archive Millennium Award Scheme'

ISBN 1-904102-03-4

Copies of this book are made available through the Nottinghamshire County Libraries and the Nottingham City Libraries. This publication contains extracts from oral history interviews; full transcripts and audio recordings of these Interviews are also available at selected libraries. Copies of the book may be available to purchase from the author. Please contact the Local Studies Department of the Central Library, Angel Row, Nottingham, NG1 6HP for further details.

Whilst every care has been taken to ensure the accuracy of the information contained in this publication, Nottinghamshire Living History Archive Millennium Award Scheme cannot accept any responsibility for any error or omission. Attempts have been made to contact copyright holders where appropriate. If any have been inadvertently missed out, this will be rectified in future editions.

Printed by Blue Print Mansfield Tel: 01623 626336 Email: enquiries@blueprintonline.co.uk

Contents

Preface

Anyone under the misconception that retirement equates to boredom, should think again. Retirement for us, the authors, is a time for pursuing all those hobbies and interests that have had to take a back seat during our working lives.

We are two friends who share many interests, one of which is a fascination with local history. We discovered the Nottinghamshire Living History Archive Millennium Award Scheme almost by accident. The final promotional talk was to be held in Newark on the very afternoon that Hilda heard of the scheme.

What she learned at that meeting in Newark determined her to apply, and to use as a theme the memories of people who had spent their childhood in Bingham during the course of the twentieth century. It was then an easy matter to interest Catherine, whose first contribution was to put a title to the project.

Having agonised over the application form, we were apprehensive at the interview, but truly delighted when the project was accepted on 21st November 2000. We were allowed eight months in which to complete the project.

Our training and instruction commenced, enabling us to meet our fellow awardees, and hear about their varied and interesting projects. We found the training to be more involved and intensive than we had expected, but very enjoyable.

We have to thank the following people for their comprehensive, patient and engrossing tuition: Joan Bray, Chris Weir and Sue Clayton for historical research, Fred Hayward, Denis Hill and Phil Sellers for tuition in the use of the equipment, Sander Meredeen for writing and editing techniques, and Judy Kingscott and Jane Foley for interviewing procedures. Their help and patience in trying to turn complete 'greenhorns' into competent living history researchers was boundless and greatly appreciated.

We are also grateful to the staff of Central Library on Angel Row, the Nottingham Archives on Canalside, and Bingham Library, all of whom have been extremely helpful.

Last, but not least, we must mention our mentors:

Denis Hill especially, has given his time, encouragement and expertise unstintingly. On his shoulders most particularly, the success of the scheme as a whole must depend.

Samantha Holgate-Davey has been indispensable in making sure our administration and budgets are in order, and in her general help and support.

This book makes no claim to be a comprehensive study of 20th Century Bingham. The time factor which limited the amount of background studying we were able to do and the number of people we were able to interview, precludes that, but in the course of a delightful, sometimes surprising project, we have made many friends, learned a lot, and had a thoroughly enjoyable time. We hope that children in future generations will find it interesting, and maybe get a better insight of life in the Twentieth Century.

Catherine Haynes

The Authors

Hilda Smith

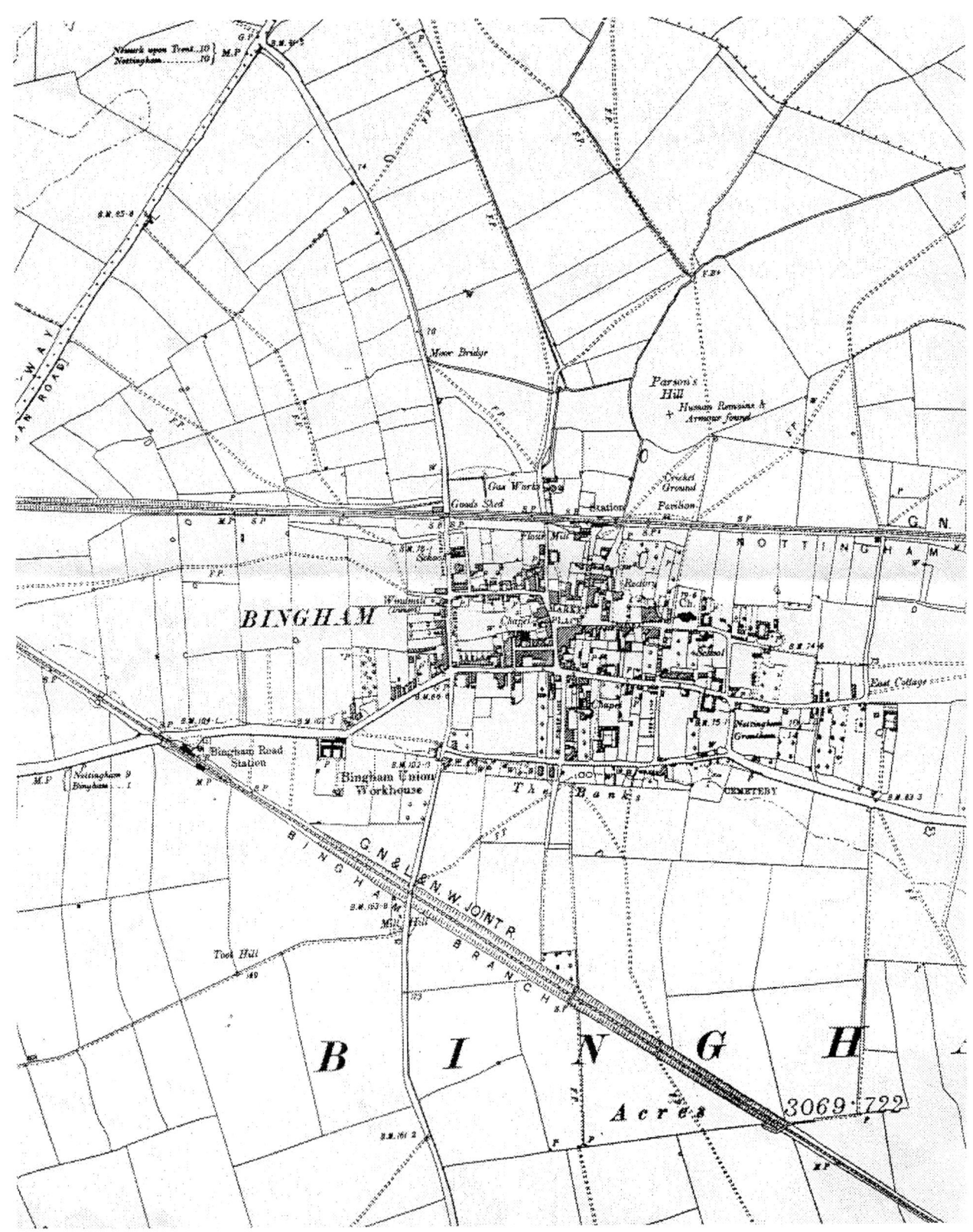

Map of Bingham - 1901

Introduction

'Change is not made without inconvenience, even from worse to better'. So said Samuel Johnson in his preface to the English Dictionary.

'Bingham's Children' sets out to describe the changes that Bingham has undergone throughout the Twentieth Century, particularly how those changes affected the lives of its children.

So how did we come to produce this book?

The Nottinghamshire Living History Archive (NLHA) set up a Millennium Award Scheme to record the memories of the last century. Oral history, first-hand accounts of what life was really like are invaluable and irreplaceable nuggets of information. Many children listen enthralled to their grandparents describing how life used to be. Many parents wish those memories had been recorded.

We have interviewed twenty five people from the ages of ninety-four down to eleven to find out what each generation's childhood was like. This book is a result of these interviews together with a lot of research.

The Archive Office in Nottingham is a goldmine of information. It holds the school logbooks of both the Church and the County (or Council) schools, also the minutes of Bingham Rural District Council meetings, Parish Records, Trade Directories and many other tomes too numerous and too time-consuming to consult.

We were given eight months to complete our project so have had to limit our studies to six themes – Environment, Home life, School life, Recreation, the War Years and Religion. The time constraint also curtailed the depth to which we could research these subjects so, enthralling though they are, we have not been able to dig as deeply as we would have wished.

We would have liked to record the memories of many more people both young and old, for everyone has a fascinating tale to tell, but again, time was against us. Apologies to those people whom we were unable to interview, and grateful thanks to the following who shared their memories with us:

Lottie Castledine (aged 94) can remember quite vividly her childhood on Starnhill Farm and has a particular memory of the First World War.

Mary Cowling (94) describes her schools and friends and recalls singing solo in the Chapel on the day our present queen was born.

Dot Mabbott (86) was born, and still lives, in Ebenezer House on The Banks. She can name all the little shops around the Market Square when she was a child.

As can **George Singleton** (83), who excelled at arithmetic at school, but left to become a farm labourer. He relates with relish the pranks he used to get up to.

Kathleen Selby (84) whose mother had to send a telegram to call the midwife when she was born because there were no telephones. She recalls the cruel winters and the agony of chilblains.

Hubert Marriott (80) was taken into the Cottage Home at the age of six and found the loss of freedom difficult to bear. Sometimes he would sneak over the wall to visit his grandparents.

Chig Pacey (71) was ten years old when the Second World War broke out. His recollections make enthralling reading.

Freda Hayes and Joyce Simpson (66 and 64) are sisters. They lived in a Council house on Stanhope Way and had an air-raid shelter at the bottom of their garden in which they played.

Margaret Smith (64) recalls regular sing-songs around the piano, with her Grandma playing and her Granddad on the cornet.

Robert Selby (60) was born at West Bank on Kirk Hill. He was known as 'the inventor' because he was always thinking up mad schemes, some of which worked.

Vida Smith (59) lived on Long Acre Row, an area demolished in the 1956 Clearance Scheme. It is now Chestnut Avenue.

Sally Wattam (59) was born on Union Street in a house built in 1694, now a listed building. Her father was a butcher.

Derrick Groombridge (57) joined the Boxing Club in 1957 and has been involved with the club ever since.

John Morris (55) was also a butcher's son. At the age of eleven he had to make the sausage meat when he got home from school.

Jane Harding (45) born in 1956, remembers sheep being driven down Fairfield Street before the traffic lights were installed.

Barry Stewart (43) loves sport and represented his school at rugby, cricket, football, athletics and cross-country.

Lindsay Smith (35) attended Toot Hill School when equality of the sexes was just beginning. She made a telephone stand in the woodwork class but girls did not yet play football.

Karen Douglass (33) describes the teenage fashions of the 1980s, from pixie boots to the 'Goths'.

Ben Selby (25) remembers cycling with his friends to the River Trent and jumping into the river with an inflated tractor inner tube round his waist.

Peter Ball (17) relished the challenge that moving from the Primary school to a large Comprehensive presented.

Manwai Yeung (16) came to Bingham from Hong Kong in 1990 and has the double pleasure of celebrating the Chinese New Year as well as Christmas.

Amy Balchin (13) thinks there are not enough facilities for younger children in Bingham. She likes swimming, disco dancing and shopping.

Joanna Hart (13) lives on Brewsters Close and has a large group of friends. They meet in each other's houses rather than in the town or across the fields.

Laura Ball (11) swims for the County. She trains nearly every day and hopes to swim in the Olympics.

Having introduced our interviewees, we hope you will enjoy their memories and insights into their lifestyles.

We have met many people, made new friends and have discovered fascinating facts about Bingham.

It has been an honour to be part of the NLHA Millennium Award Scheme and to produce this book, 'Bingham's Children of the Twentieth Century'.

Chapter I – The Environment

'When I was a child all the Council estate was fields. We used to play right across there, right across the cricket field and Parson's Hill, there was no industrial site there, the Church Farm estate was all fields, Frank Nicholson's farmhouse was the last house through Church Street. The houses along Grantham Road as far as Derry Lane were there but behind them and right down to the railway were all fields where we used to play'. So says John Morris, describing Bingham in his childhood.

As you drive into Bingham today from the Saxondale crossroads, past the extensive housing estates which sprawl both sides of the road, it is difficult to imagine how different the scene was at the beginning of the Twentieth Century. The neat detached and semi-detached houses and bungalows, nestling amongst the trees and well-tended gardens, suggest an air of well-established prosperity. Gone are the rolling fields of grass and corn, the cherished and flourishing allotments and orchards of former years.

The railway bridge, which once stood like a gateway, and Stanhope House, a forbidding edifice which marked the western edge of Bingham, have also disappeared.

The bridge, once part of the Nottingham-Melton Mowbray railway line, was blown up in the sixties. Stanhope House was the Union Workhouse where 'old men and tramps were obliged to break stones for road-mending' in exchange for food and shelter, and every occupant had to work towards its upkeep. Later it was transformed into an Old Peoples' Home but was pulled down in 1964. Maybe the stigma of its former purpose could not be expunged.

Stanhope House

Closer to the centre of the town you come across the Victorian and Edwardian villas of the former professional classes. These solid examples of prosperity have stood the test of time, showing little change on the outside, but inwardly have been converted to include all the modern conveniences of today.

Very few of the old terraced cottages and houses, which once abounded in Bingham, still remain. Most of them survived the first half of the century, for very little changed in the village during that period. They were mostly concentrated in streets surrounding the Market Place or situated in 'rows' behind the grander houses on Long Acre. They were occupied by the poorer classes – farm labourers, estate workers, domestic servants, tailors, seamstresses, etc. These terraces had small gardens or, more likely yards, but many of the occupants rented allotments to grow fruit and vegetables.

In 1956 there was a Grand Clearance Scheme which saw the demolition of most of the old terrace blocks, Long Acre Row, Chancel Row, Morris Row, Escort Place and Chapel Yard being some which disappeared altogether. They were obviously considered by the Council to be too old and dilapidated to be renovated and were torn down to make way for more modern establishments – or car parks.

Long Acre from Nottingham Road

Derrick Groombridge: *'No. 1 Needham Street…in a row of terraced houses…it was very old, I'm really surprised they actually knocked it down and made just a car park. If they'd done it like Newark, like a museum, people'd be going round there saying what a lovely place it was.'*

Escort Place

Acre Row Clearance 1956

The Market Square was the hub of the village – for village it was in those days – with dozens of small shops in the square and surrounding streets.

Market Place

Until 1962 the square was rough ground with a track crossing diagonally from Market Street to Station Street. Early in the century Sunday school outings and other parades would congregate there and set off round the village, led by the Bingham Brass Band.

On Boxing Day the South Notts Hunt would meet, and Dot Mabbott remembers the two Miss Marriotts, who ran the telephone exchange, taking a tray of drinks out to the huntsmen.

There was an annual fair held in the Market Place – cakewalks, swings, round-abouts and sideshows, and the caravans as well, on the Church Street side.

The population of Bingham in 1901 was 1,604, but in spite of a slight decline to 1,587 in 1931 the needs of the small community seem to have been amply provided for. In effect, Bingham was almost self-sufficient as Kelly's Trade Directory of 1928 illustrates. It lists the following shops and businesses:

4 Public Houses, 1 furniture dealer, 3 greengrocers, 3 boot/shoe dealers and 2 bootmakers, 1 joiner, 1 cycle agent, 2 general clothing and household suppliers, 4 butchers, 1 seedsman, 2 painter/decorators, 2 plumbers, 1 fried fish shop, 4 general grocers, 1 newsagent, 1 watchmaker, 2 drapers, 1 hairdresser, 1 hardware shop, 1 Post Office, 1 tailor, 2 bakers, 1 Bank, 1 Welfare Centre, 1 chemist, 1 confectioner, 1 saddler, 1 blacksmith, 1 builder, and 1 'tin man'. Presumably he was a tin man by profession, not an adjunct to a scarecrow and a lion.

Several others were listed merely as shopkeepers.

Sunday School Parade

Also listed as businesses, on East Street was a smallholder, on Long Acre a farmer and a threshing machine proprietor, on Union Street a butcher and cow keeper and, location unspecified, a castrator.

Many of the most affluent members of the community were farmers, whose land, buildings and farmyards formed an integral part of the village, as well as embracing the surrounding countryside.

As well as farming, Bingham was noted for its orchards. All the people we have interviewed who remember Bingham in the first half of the century recall the orchards and fruit production. *'Bingham was all orchards,* Kathleen Selby reflected, *'along The Banks, there were all orchards, and under the trees grew daffodils and hyacinths and all sorts of snowdrops at the start. And Mrs. Baker's, right at the corner of Grantham Road, and opposite Parry's there was an orchard. They're all houses now. The family orchard my grandfather planted...he reckoned to make the year's rent (for the Post Office and orchard) out of his plums, apples, greengage – every type of apple.'*

Bingham from Mill Hill early 1900s

Freda Hayes: *'My grandparent's farm on East Street...they grew every kind of fruit. Gran used to sort the plums, apples, pears and greengage into trays to be collected by Nottingham people.'*

Even in the sixties Barry Stewart recalls, *'We had, to the west side of Bingham up towards Saxondale roundabout, a great big orchard called Smith's orchard and there were rows and rows of fruit trees and we used to go in there and get the fruit. And there was another orchard on The Banks where we used to 'borrow' the apples and pears.'*

So, we can appreciate that Bingham, for more than half of the century was a small, almost self-sufficient village abounding with orchards, green spaces and farm buildings – a perfect habitat for children to grow up in.

Aerial View of Market Place early 1950s

11

But not everything was ideal. Other factors can affect the environment of a community, such as provision of the utilities - water, gas and electricity and telephones. Bingham appeared to be behind the times in obtaining these services.

It was only in the 1930s that new water mains were laid from Nottingham by the County Council, and electricity cables supplied by the Notts and Derbys Electricity Company.

Up till then all water was obtained from wells. Only the methods of extraction were different.

'We had no running water, we had a pump outside for drinking water and a pump over the sink for soft water…this water ran off the roof into a cistern under the kitchen floor.' This must have seemed quite a modern innovation when Dot Mabbott's father built their house. But it was a different matter in the row of small cottages on Needham Street where Derrick Groombridge lived. *'Every house had a well…but we didn't have a winder to wind the bucket down, you just got a rope and threw the bucket down.'* He also said, *'There were gas lamps…so it was usually dark and it was how much gas you used and how much it cost was whether the lights went on or not. And there were gas lamps on the street which somebody would come round and light.'*

It was 1950 when John Morris, aged five, moved with his parents to the cottage on Long Acre. *'There was no running water, there were pumps and troughs, no electricity, there were oil lamps hanging from the beams.'*

Sally Wattam: *'Most people had a pump in their backyard and also a wash-house and a coal-place.'*

Kelly's Trade Directory of 1941 states: 'the town is lighted with gas, the water supply is obtained from wells and also from the Corporation of Nottingham. Electricity is available'. But not to every house. It was available mainly to houses on the main thoroughfares.

Old cottages – Chapel Yard

Even as late as 1946 a letter in the minutes of a Bingham Rural District Council meeting stated, 'Before approval can be given to any proposed layout of a housing site the Department will require evidence that a local supply of water exists on the site. Where wells are to be used it is essential that the well….should be tested for quality and quantity.'

Gas for lighting and cooking was supplied by the local Bingham Gas Company until nationalisation of the industry after the Second World War.

Coal fires were the usual method of domestic heating, often supplemented by coke from the Gas Works.

The telegraph service was available from the Post Office, but the telephone exchange, operated from a small house on the south side of the Market Place, did not arrive until the late 1920s. There is an entry in the Council School logbook dated 25th January 1927 saying that a 'wire' notifying postponement of an inspection was not received at the school until 12.30pm on Tuesday although it had been received at the Post Office the previous afternoon.

The first few Council houses were built on Tythby Road and Long Acre in 1929 but it was after the Second World War, in the late 1940s, that housing development really started to take off. Slowly at first, beginning with land acquired by the Council for the building of more 'Housing for the Working Classes' on the western side of the village, followed later in the 1950s by the first large private estate at Garden Road.

Council House 1929

On the eastern side, in 1959 fifteen and a half acres of land were pinpointed for private development by J Enness and Co. By 1964, more than 400 houses had been built on the Church Farm and Holme Farm Estates and further developments on Grantham Road were in the pipeline.

By the end of 1968 the population had grown to over 4000. To cope with the growing number of children two Primary schools and one Comprehensive were built, closely followed by the first Sports and Leisure Centre in the country.

Shopping facilities did not keep pace with the growing population. It was not until September 1977 that Eaton Place shopping precinct was completed. But many of the little shops had already gone out of business, either pulled down to make way for more modern concerns or unable to compete with the out-of-town supermarkets and shopping malls. By this time most families had a car.

As private cars and heavy-goods vehicles multiplied over the years the roads also had to be improved. And as the roads were improved so the vehicles increased. The traffic through the narrow, winding main road of Bingham became dangerously excessive. A new by-pass was constructed in 1987 – 'the best thing that ever happened to Bingham' was how residents greeted the opening in June. But the A46 and A52 today are still seriously congested at peak times.

Bingham has continued to grow to the west as far as Saxondale island, to the south right up to the by-pass and to the east along Grantham Road, but the barrier of the railway line to the north has precluded further housing development so far. 2000 new houses were programmed for that area under the County Structure Plan in 1996 but that plan was overturned – for the time being. The demand for housing grows continually. No longer are there green spaces and everlasting fields, as described in the opening paragraph of this chapter, for Bingham's children to play in and roam over. The playing field and Parson's Hill are still available, and provision for small play areas have been included in the latest estates, but previously, no consideration was given to this matter at all.

Aerial View of Bingham late 1960s

We can see how physically, Bingham has altered over the last century – which is all due to man's ingenuity and progress – but what about a factor which seems beyond man's control?

When asked about their memories of winter we got the same response from all our older interviewees - much colder, much more severe. They talked about a lot more snow, and ice on ponds and streams which was thick enough to skate on.

Chig Pacey: *'They were good, there was snow in those days. We used to have a sledge, Bluebird we called it, and of course, where the school is now, the hollow was ideal for sledging, and some of the more adventurous boys used to sledge down the embankment to the railway lines.'*

Dot Mabbott remembers them as *'very cold and the houses were very cold...we just had coal fires and we had to pull up to the fire to keep warm.'*

Joyce Simpson: *'We used to go sledging down those hills* (Mill Hill) *when it was really bad, or the fields. And we used to have a really great time because there weren't many cars, they couldn't get up the hill when it was bad, so we used to start at the top and go right down.'*

George Singleton: *'Plenty of snowballs...they went lots of places, especially if you saw someone walking past with a trilby on. Half the school would have a go at the trilby.'*

Kathleen Selby had *'chilblains. I remember having to stay at home because I could get neither shoes nor boots on my feet.'*

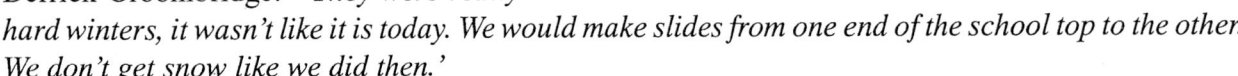

Floods - Kirk Hill 1920s

Derrick Groombridge: *'They were really hard winters, it wasn't like it is today. We would make slides from one end of the school top to the other. We don't get snow like we did then.'*

Margaret Smith: *'I can remember particularly when I had to go on the bus to school, after it had snowed that the drifts were that high the bus only went as far as the bottom of Saxondale Hill and we used to have to walk the rest of the way home. But it was fun.'*

Floods – Main Road 1947

Jane Harding: *'I can remember there being ice on the inside of the windows in the winter.'*

As well as snow and ice there were often floods to contend with. Fairfield Street was formerly Pond Street. A pond on the east side often overflowed and made the roadway impassable. Later it was drained and filled in. There are frequent references in the school logbooks to absences of children from outlying areas due to 'heavy rain causing flooding'.

In 1967 there was a freak storm of hail and rain which flooded nearly every street and road in Bingham.

The winters were recalled as being definitely much harder than those of today and the summers were apparently much hotter and longer, born out by memories of long hours playing in the fields and helping with harvests. It is only in recent years that sunshine has been deemed to be dangerous and skin block has to be applied. Whether this is due to global warming or other factors has yet to be decided, but pollution of the atmosphere, resulting in thinning of the ozone layer, is the favoured belief at the moment.

The extensive development and changes in all aspects of environment over the last hundred years have provided both advantages and disadvantages for children growing up in Bingham.

Today's children have better housing, motor cars, foreign holidays, a milder climate and the Sports Centre.

Peter Ball: '*I think the Sports Centre is very good but it doesn't cater for children particularly well...apart from that I don't think there is much else.*'

Amy Balchin: '*Bingham's OK but there's not a lot of facilities, there's not a lot of shops that younger children would like to go to. The Leisure Centre has good things but the swimming pools are a bit boring.*'

In contrast, the memories of people born in the first half of the century, even up to the 1960s, are more positive.

Jane Harding: '*Growing up in my teens, there did seem enough to do because our expectations weren't very high. We used to go down to the Wash Pit, down Moor Lane, fishing for tiddlers and things like that.*'

Derrick Groombridge: '*It is a different childhood today, different to what we had. I don't think the money was about...I really enjoyed my childhood.*'

John Morris: '*I'm sad to see how Bingham has changed, I don't think it's for the better.*'

Chig Pacey: '*Well, I think to be honest, it's completely ruined the place. When I was young we never used to have to lock doors, everybody was honest. You could walk across the fields to the Fosse, no houses...and all the little shops have gone.*'

George Singleton: '*Actually, I think it was better in those days. We wasn't so well off but what we did have, we enjoyed.*'

Dot Mabbott: '*Well, my childhood was very happy and there was no stress in those days, as they call it. They're worn out by stress but I never knew anyone stressed out in those days...we just lived a happy life.*'

Robert Selby: '*There was never any boredom, we could always do with extra money and more technology, but by and large, I haven't got anything to grumble about at all. I enjoyed it.*'

Physical advantages of improved housing, better roads and transport, modern utilities, technology in schools, etc., cannot always compensate for the freedom and innocence of childhood in years gone by. But the children of today don't miss what they have never had.

Bingham will continue to expand and develop, housing estates will continue to be built, hopefully with a little more thought and consideration for the residents, particularly the children, than has been shown in the past. But it will keep growing. That's progress.

Grantham Road Estate 2000

The Buttercross in the early 1960s

Chapter II - Home Life

'*A*cross *a yard, the old lavatory pan. No toilets like they have today. The old lavatory pan that was emptied once a week by one of the farmers'*.

George Singleton describing the only toilet facilities available in most Bingham houses at the beginning of the twentieth century.

Our oldest contributor, Lottie Castledine, lived on Starnhill Farm as a child. Lottie was born in 1907 and had two brothers and two sisters. Starnhill Farm was a six bed-roomed farmhouse, which she describes as being 'quite big'. Two big kitchens, two staircases, one at the front and the other out of the kitchen: *'The back stairs, up where the men used to sleep.'*

So the family shared their home with the farm workers.

Six bedrooms but no bathroom. In one kitchen was the oven and the range, which had a hot water tap attached. The other kitchen contained the copper and was

Starnhill Farm

where they did all the work and butter-making. There were two rooms at the front, and the house was lit by candles and lamps. The toilet was located right around the house and nearly into the orchard:

Lottie: 'But of course, upstairs you had the chambers' *(chamberpots)*.

Another of our children of the earlier part of the twentieth century is Dot Mabbott. Dot was a child in the twenties and her house, Ebenezer House, was built by her father with the help of one workman.

Dot Mabbott: *'There wasn't a lot of money about in those days, and in the bible, Ebenezer means help, and I think that's why my father called it Ebenezer, because I think he thought the Lord would help him.'*

They had no running water, but a pump outside for drinking water. Water running off the roof was collected in a cistern underneath the kitchen floor and pumped from there to the kitchen sink.

John Morris describing his cottage: *'It was wooden and stone floors; there was no running water; there was pumps and troughs;*

Ebenezer House

no electricity; there was oil lamps [hanging] from the centre of the beams. I can remember getting up in the morning and scraping frost off the upstairs windows. There wasn't even a bathroom. There was an outside toilet which the Bingham wagons came round and emptied.'

The cottage is quite modern inside now, although John is still in some danger of cracking his head on the low ceilings and old beams. Outside it has retained all of its original charm and character.

Another house of particular interest, but on the outskirts of Bingham, is Buggins Cottage. It was occupied during his childhood, by Chig Pacey's grandparents. His grandfather was a gamekeeper for Lord Carnarvon, and they lived there for thirty years. Chig liked to drink the water there:

'It came from a spring across the road, a fresh water spring, which the doctor said was far better than the stuff we get out of the taps now.'

Buggins Cottage

Mains water will doubtless have been put in since then. One of the cottage's more recent owners, was Dennis McCarthy MBE, a well-known and respected presenter for Radio Nottingham until his death in 1996.

The cottage stood at Buggins Corner, where one road led to Bingham. The other, the old Fosse Way, carried on its long straight way to Lincoln in one direction, and Leicester in the other. Many Roman artefacts are to be found in the fields around Buggins Corner, it being close to the site of the old Roman garrison of Margidunum. Much of Margidunum has since been dug over to make way for a roundabout.

Chig's own house was Gordon House, originally gas lit until his father installed electricity. There was a well in the garden for drinking water. Another pump using soft water collected from the roof was used for washing. And only an outside toilet...'*there wasn't water toilets then. In fact, there wasn't water.*'

Sally Wattam, whose house is a listed building dating from 1694, describes it with pride as being a three storey house and part two storey house. It was 3 or 4 cottages knocked into one, and so has quite a lot of rooms. Upstairs there are eight bedrooms, downstairs only two rooms have been retained by the family. The others have been rented out and are used as a little cafe. All the fireplaces are original. The two panelled doors are late 1700s and the floor plan has not changed since 1800. There is a cellar where the meat was salted years ago.

This old house, beautifully restored by English Heritage, was no place of comfort when Sally was growing up. Sally, who was a child in the forties and fifties, says that they did have electric lighting, but no hot water. There was an old-fashioned leaded fireplace with an oven and boiler, and they would ladle the hot water out of the boiler. The house did have a bathroom, but the bath was very 'old-fashioned'. However, they seemed to have had an ingenious system for pumping hot water up from the copper in the wash house to the bathroom upstairs. Then in order to cool the water, an empty bucket was lowered by rope through a trap door, filled with cold water and hauled back up to the bathroom.

George Singleton lived at the bottom end of Kirkhill, near the railway line.

'*It was two houses knocked into one. We had four bedrooms. A family of about ten, apart from my father and mother. Ten brothers and sisters.*'

George remembers that there was gas lighting, no hot water, but a pump in the yard and a well. There was an old lavatory pan across a yard, emptied every week by one of the farmers, and an old black stove and a copper in the kitchen. Water for a bath was boiled in the copper, and the bath taken once a week in an old zinc tub in front of the fire in the kitchen. The copper was also used to cook the Christmas puddings; as many as a dozen at a time.

Kathleen Selby also lived in Union Street - in fact, next door to Sally's house, but from an earlier period in the century.

Kathleen: '*A nice little house next to the butcher's shop....It was a double-fronted house, had a couple of steps up to the front door. There was a dining room one side, and a sitting room the other, a kitchen at the back. Unfortunately there was only a yard.......I think there were about four bedrooms, probably on two flights.'*

Some houses were better equipped than others. The house that Robert Selby lived in as a child in the 1940s, was a semi-detached, large Victorian house on Kirkhill.

Robert: *'That used to be the Minister's house when there was a church on Kirkhill.'*

It had running water, flushing toilet and a bath - very modern for the time and very different from the back to back farm labourers' cottages nearby.

In one of these Hubert Marriott lived, until the tragic events that overtook his young life. His mother became ill enough to be taken to hospital, and at age seven, he was left with no one to care for him. It was therefore decided by the good people of the parish, that he should be housed in the local Cottage Homes.

The Cottage Homes were used as accommodation for young children whose parents were temporarily unable to care for them. The parents themselves were often housed in the local workhouse, Stanhope House. Mothers about to give birth were taken there if their homes were unsuitable, which they often were. The Cottage Homes would then accommodate any other children in the family until such time as mother and baby were fit to return home.

Hubert remembers little of these unhappy times, but does remember sleeping with other children in one large room, and there being at least one bathroom. The bath had to be filled by buckets of water being carried up to it. The lavatories were the usual kind in Bingham at that time, as Hubert has good cause to remember.

In the early part of the century, many Bingham children lived in rows of small cottages, and living accommodation was cramped in the extreme; it being quite usual for there to be five children in a house with two bedrooms, or a family of ten housed in a four bed-roomed house.

Old Eto's ghost haunted just such a house on Needham Street. Derrick Groombridge, who lived there as a child in the 1940s, is very sad that this row of old houses was demolished in the 1960s.

He feels that if the old houses in Needham Street had been saved, they would be a tourist attraction now, as are some of the old houses in Newark.

It is doubtful, however, if these houses *could* have

Needham Street

been saved. They were built, in the main, with no proper foundations, with just dirt or brick floors, and were probably too far gone to repair.

Old Eto's ghost would certainly have proved a point of interest on any tourist trail, but unfortunately no one seems to know his story, or *why* he decided to haunt the house. Old Eto had lived in the house, and had carried on his trade as a tailor there. One room downstairs had a big shop window, and one imagines him sitting there, cross-legged, plying his trade. Derek says that the front door bell would ring promptly at six o' clock each day, and everyone would say 'That's old Eto's ghost'.

The street outside was lit by gaslight, but the passageway between the kitchen-cum-living room and the room with the shop window, was nevertheless very dark, and Derrick used to hurtle through to his mother in the kitchen, gabbling, *'The ghost didn't get me, the ghost didn't get me'*. Some of the family may have found it quite amusing, but the terror of 'old Eto', probably loomed quite large in Derrick's young life. Now he says, *'I don't believe in ghosts, but that's what my mother'd tell you - It was haunted.'*

Later, when they moved to Tythby Road, he paints a wonderful picture of the old bath in the kitchen, which, with a board on top, served as a seat for the children of the family when not in use as a bath. As the children got older, they were promoted to a proper chair

Even by the 1940s, home life for many was extremely uncomfortable by today's standards. Very often houses had no mains water or electricity. However, when everyone is suffering the same hardships, they somehow seem not to be so bad. Nevertheless, interviewees give a distinct impression of the relief they felt when the joint blessings of electric light and mains water finally came to *all* in Bingham.

Vida Smith, child of the 1940s, on moving to a Council house: *'To actually turn on a tap in the house and have hot water coming out of it! I remember promising my Mum that I would always wash the pots - I don't think I did, but I can remember promising it.'*

Joyce Simpson and Freda Hayes, also lived in a Council house. Freda describes it as, *'Just a little Council house...we had one big kitchen, and one big room and three bedrooms'*. There was a bathroom downstairs, and they had electric light and coal fires.

By the time Barry Stewart was born in 1958, things had begun to improve, inasmuch as most people had mains water and electricity, but he still remembers waking up to frost on the inside of the windows upstairs, and running downstairs to get dressed for school in front of the fire.

Jane Harding, remembers with affection the house in which she was born in Fairfield Street. At that time, the house had solid fuel stoves called 'Tall Glows' - two of them downstairs. No heating upstairs at all. Jane, who is just a couple of years younger than Barry, remembers that her bedroom was very small and also very cold in winter. It faced towards the square.

'And there was an allotment where the car park for the Health Centre is now, so it was actually very peaceful looking back over towards old Bingham.'

Jane seems to remember her little bedroom with some affection, although she does describe conditions in the house as, *'quite spartan really, compared to these days'*. Her bedroom had 'lino' on the floor *'that my Mum used to dry mop and collect all the dust.'* And a *'very old bed with a feather mattress that had a nice comfortable dip in it.'*

Today's children, by contrast, now live in the most comfortable surroundings. Joanna Hart, aged thirteen, describes her house as a four bed-roomed semi with many modern gadgets: dishwasher, washing machine, television and microwave - very modern and nicely decorated throughout.

Most houses these days are very well appointed. Many people own their own homes, and take good care of them. They take great pride in the appearance of their houses, both inside and out, and spend quite a large proportion of their income on maintaining both house and garden.

Laura Ball, aged eleven, describes her house as a reasonably big, four bedroomed house in a quiet cul-de-sac. It has a kitchen, a living room, bathroom and loo, and one of the bedrooms has an en suite shower and loo. Her brother, Peter, speaks of the large garden at the back, which backs onto fields.

Manwai Yeung and Amy Balchin live in similar houses to these. Amy says her house has three bedrooms, bathroom and toilet together, large lounge and a dining room off the kitchen, a fairly large back garden, a garage and a front garden. The house is centrally heated.

Manwai's house has three bedrooms, an upstairs toilet, kitchen, dining room and lounge, and is double-glazed and centrally heated. There is a garden which Manwai describes as not very big and *'not very neat either'*, although it does have a couple of pear trees. It is probably true to say that no one in the family has time or inclination to take a great interest in the garden.

So these children are living in homes that are designed to be as comfortable as possible, with double-glazing and central heating to ensure warmth, and all modern labour-saving gadgets to ensure that the house is easily kept clean. In addition, manufacturers produce enough variety of furniture, fabrics, paint and wallpaper to enable them to have a house furnished to suit their own individual tastes.

They may not be as individual in design as the old village houses used to be, and ghosts would probably not find all that light and electrical equipment conducive to a good haunting. But children of today seem very happy to be living in them.

The parents of children in the early part of the century would have worked long and hard for little money. Few mothers had jobs outside the home. They may have worked on the farm or gone out cleaning in addition to their work in the house, but this would not be considered a 'job' as women have jobs these days. In the case of a farmer's wife, it was seen as merely additional domestic chores. For the woman going out cleaning, it may have meant the difference between eating or not, for her family. How all those women worked!

Lottie Castledine used to help her mother in the house and on the farm, so she would know exactly how hard her mother worked. They would see to the poultry and collect about a hundred eggs a day. Tuesday was washday, and they would be washing nearly all day. There was a brick copper with a fire under it to boil all the whites, and a dolly tub, (a labour-saving device of the time). *'Then we had starch, blue bags for the rinsing.... A bowl of starch for those*

Lottie's mother feeding the poultry

things that wanted starching. We used to starch every tablecloth...and pillow cases and things like that. All white stuff that was linen. Then on Wednesday there was all the ironing to do when it dried.' The ironing was done with flat irons heated on the fire. On Thursday they cleaned all upstairs; Friday, all downstairs.

Her father managed the farm for Hardstaff and Brown, who had a big grocer's shop in the village. Doubtless he worked extremely hard too:

Lottie: *'Didn't have any tractors... used to take the horses round to cut the corn. Used to take the wagons and pick it up and bring it back to make a stack in the yard.'*

Starnhill Farm Bull

Just like farming folk today, they would become very attached to their animals. Lottie tells us that the bull got anthrax and *'had to be burned and they dug a big hole in the field - it was terrible'*. Even after all these years, it remains a vivid memory for Lottie.

George Singleton's father worked at Walker's Drill Works on Nottingham Road, making farm machinery. His job was that of 'blacksmith's striker'. He had a wooden leg, to replace one that he had lost when it got caught in a grass cutter.

When the catastrophe happened, he was mowing a meadow at Barnstone, using a horse-drawn mower. He got off to clear the blade, and forgot to put the machine out of gear. At the same time:

'Some damn fool come down with an aeroplane, straight over the top of the horses.'

The horses ran away, of course, and he got his leg caught fast, and the blade cut it off. How he survived is a miracle. It must have been hard on all the family until he recovered sufficiently to return to work. No compensation in those days, and probably no sick pay either.

George's mother used to have dried peas delivered from Batchelor's factory in East Bridgford, as did many of the women. Eighteen stone sacks of peas at a time. She had to sort them out and pick out the bad ones. This 'home-work' may have helped the family survive, during the time his father was unable to work.

Whilst men were recognised for the jobs they did, often women's only reward for hard work, was the satisfaction of knowing that they were doing their best for the family.

Mary Cowling, 94 years old told us that they were a family of ten. When asked what her Mum and Dad did, she replied, '*My Dad was a butcher - my mother didn't work because of the children.*'

With ten children in the family and none of the labour-saving devices we have today, it seems strange that women were ever described as 'not working'. In those days, a woman's work truly was 'never done'.

Vida Smith's father worked in Bingham as a saddler for a time, but later he went to work for Smith Englefield in Nottingham and stayed there for fifty-two years. When he left, he was presented with a gold watch and a garden seat.

Freda Hayes's and Joyce Simpson's father worked for Doncaster's. He drove a van all around the little villages. People would buy their goods on credit, and pay for them so much a week. Before that, he was in the army in France. He missed his wife and daughters very much, and sent them presents of dainty little silk handkerchiefs.

Derrick Groombridge's father was in the army too, and served his time in Burma.

Derrick: '*When he was here, it was quite busy in that house.*'

Derrick's mother took in lodgers, and he tells us that at one time there were five children, two adults and three lodgers all living in a three bed-roomed house.

Margaret Smith's father was in the army, and then worked as a farm labourer. As she says: '*There wasn't much money about*'. She was an only child, however, so at least her parents would not have had to stretch the money as far as some others may have done.

Dot Mabbott describes her father as a 'jobbing builder'. If that means someone who can do any job involved with building, then that must be right. He built his own house, after all.

Sally Wattam's mother seems to have been the main breadwinner for her family. It was she and her elder daughter who ran the butcher's shop in Union Street. Poor Sally just hated wash days. It was the same day that the animals were slaughtered: '*Wet floors, washing and cold meat. I just hated Mondays.*'

Chig Pacey followed in his father's footsteps as a motor engineer, but during the war his father was on Nottinghamshire's War Agricultural Executive Committee – '*as a sort of Manager or whatever.*'

In the early days, John Morris's father worked as salesman in menswear in Nottingham:

They used to have to wear bowler hats and stiff, separate collars.

He would bicycle in to Nottingham to work each day. Before her marriage, his mother worked in Boots, but the whole family also worked as butchers, and kept pigs in the back yard.

Robert Selby says that his father did lots of different things. He was in the army, then worked for WarAg,

J Enness Company building

'*delivering large agricultural machinery to farms on a loan basis, to get the farms back [into production] after the war.*' Then he went to the Gas Board, then worked for himself under contract to the Council.

Barry Stewart's father was a builder, and worked for a company that was based in a handsome building next to the church in East Street. This was J Enness and Company, and its owner and Managing Director, Mr Colin McLeod, was responsible for many of the new estates that began springing up in Bingham in the 1960s.

Barry's mother was a kitchen helper at the Infant School, and Jane Harding's Mum when she first returned to work, began as a 'lollipop lady', standing on duty at a school crossing patrol point, to ensure that children crossed the road in safety. This was typically, the sort of part-time work undertaken by women at that time, as they began to move from the home back into the work place.

Ben Selby's father, Philip, is a landscape gardener. His mother, unusually for these days, does not work outside of the home.

The mining industry having been decimated in the last decades of the century, Laura and Peter Ball's father, who works as a miner in Mansfield, must be one of the few left, or as Peter says, *'bit of a dying breed'*. Their mother is a nurse in the Queen's Medical Centre in Nottingham. The children are obviously very proud of both of them, and rightly so. Both parents have cars to enable them to get to work.

Peter: *My Dad's got a large saloon car, a Daewoo, it's about four years old. My Mum's is a Fiesta, a Ford Fiesta, and she just bought that recently.....*

Joanna Hart's father works for Severn Trent water. For a place like Bingham, which was without mains water and sewage for such a large part of the century, his work is something that the whole village will applaud and see as vitally necessary. Her mother also works outside the home as a 'mobile' hairdresser. For women in the outlying villages, she must be a very welcome visitor.

Manwai's parents both work extremely hard, helping to run a local restaurant.

Very few, if any, of the children of the first half of the century would have been given pocket money to spend. The concept would have been almost totally alien to them. For the most part they would not even have expected any payment for work done.

Children in the Cottage Homes were certainly expected to earn their keep. Not that Hubert Marriott minded hard work, even when it involved sweeping a large yard, and cleaning all the lavatories. We already know what the lavatories of the time were like, so can assume that it was not pleasant work. When not engaged in these duties, he would be expected to help with the gardening and 'pegging' (making) rugs. The girls did all the washing up and cleaning, but he had to help carry buckets of water up for the baths.

Hubert could cope with hard work, but the one thing he found it difficult to come to terms with, was his loss of freedom. No longer could he go off with his friends after school, and wander far and wide as he pleased. The only times he was allowed out, other than on organised outings, was to go to the Boys' Brigade, his one bright spot in the week. He was adequately fed, housed and clothed, but not free.

Mary Cowling, like Lottie Castledine, was one of a big family and had to help with the washing, which was done two or three times a week because, *'my father was a butcher and he must have a clean white apron every day.'*

John Morris, whose family also were butchers, was expected to work too: *'Every evening when I came home from school, I had to make sausage meat for the shop.'*

For this he was paid two shillings and sixpence a week. He earned an extra sixpence for delivering the meat.

Many of the 'children' speak of queuing for coal at the gas works, or 'Gassy Coopers', as it was known locally, a Mr Cooper being the manager at the time. Margaret Smith remembers it as a regular Saturday morning event: *'Down to the gasworks, which was over the railway crossing. I used to take an old pram and queue for bags of coke to take back home and burn on the fire.'*

George Singleton also used to collect coke, which he says was about three pence a bag. He is about twenty years older than Margaret, so it seems that this was a practice amongst Bingham people, that went on for some time. In addition, he would help with washing up and help his mother pick over the peas: *'Used to have to pick a bowlful every day before school.'*

Ben Selby had to work on his Dad's smallholding for his pocket money. He tells us that at first he did this with some reluctance, but later came to enjoy it.

For the younger generation of children, things are rather different:

Peter Ball: *'I've got a part time job. I work at Cost Cutter in Bingham, but I do get a certain amount of pocket money off my parents. I get ten pound every week for my dinners, but I also get twenty-five pounds a month for - just to spend on whatever really - at my leisure. But clothes and things like that, my Mum tends to buy for me out of the Family Allowance.'*

His sister, Laura, isn't quite as fortunate. She helps with the gardening, and sometimes with the housework. She does get pocket money, but seems to need most of it for her swimming expenses. She swims for the County, and in galas and competitions, but is still expected to pay for the time spent in the pool, training. She also has to have several swim suits, and altogether finds it quite an expensive sport. It is surprising that youngsters who show a special aptitude for a sport, aren't given more financial support.

It is good to report that throughout the twentieth century, even during the war years, most of our 'children' were fortunate enough to have eaten quite well. Many of their parents would have had friends or relations who were farmers, or they might themselves have had orchards and grown fruit. Some kept pigs, some had allotments, and so would have had fresh vegetables. Most probably, a thriving bartering system was in operation. Also there were many enterprising fellows who went out and caught the occasional rabbit or game bird.

Chig Pacey has a little grumble that will strike a chord with many of us: *'It was proper bread in those days.'* Speaking of bread from a proper coal-fired bakery: *'Bread never tasted the same since we went electric.'*

They all seem to have had good healthy appetites. Dot Mabbott says they always had a fried breakfast in those days, although *'you could have porridge... Lovely lunches because we all liked our food here.'* - Stews and roasts, and they always had a pudding.

She also remembers that they had milk brought around in a can. *'Not a churn. They carried it. I don't know whether they called them cans, milk cans. I think they did, and they had different sizes for how much milk you used to want.'*

In these days of dieting, it is good to hear food spoken of in a matter of fact way, and not as though it were something sinful. Joyce and Freda remember their mother serving *'just basic, plain good food.'* They speak with enthusiasm of *'Gran's apple dumplings,'* and of the Sunday joint, usually of beef, which was later minced and made into stews in the week. Rabbit pie they remember, and the special Sunday teatime treat of tinned fruit, which must, by the way, be eaten with bread and butter.

They remember too, there always being plenty of eggs, and during the war: *'Dried eggs for omelettes - we used to love that.'*

When asked what sort of food she ate as a child, Mary Cowling said: *'Good solid food. We always ate well.'*

Whilst it is good to hear food spoken of with relish, unfortunately not everyone can.

Boy with milk cans

Hubert Marriott: *'It was good food, but it wasn't always food that you liked. You know, you used to get a lot of fat bacon, boiled bacon. Well, I know a lot of kids didn't like it - I didn't.'*

Poor Vida Smith hated school dinners, and was made to sit in the school hall the whole of one dinner time with a plate of food she detested in front of her. *'I don't think I ever stayed school dinners after that'*, she said with some feeling. Nevertheless, she enjoyed dinners at home, which consisted of potatoes, not much meat, gravy and vegetables. Obviously, Mum knew just how Vida liked her dinners.

Margaret Smith says her mother used to do all her own baking, as many women did at that time. She also says that, her grandfather being a butcher, *'There was always a lot of meat and hams hanging from the beams in the house. So we always used to have a lot of meat and vegetables'*. Later she said that they always had a lot of fruit, so it was probably quite a healthy diet.

Unlike Barry Stewart's diet. He confesses to eating a lot of chips and very few vegetables. He just didn't like vegetables. But he did like his Mum's rice pudding. In fact the whole family did: *'Used to be a fight for it when it came out of the oven, for who was having the skin off the top.'*

Freda Hayes remembers her grandmother's rice puddings: *'She used to put big rice puddings in all night, ready for the next lunch time.'*

A recurring theme amongst these older 'children', was a love of the Sunday roast, complete with all the vegetables, and the Yorkshire puddings. Often they said that their Christmas Day meat would be a chicken or a capon, and they certainly would have enjoyed that too. But it would seem that for them, nothing compares with the 'roast beef of old England'.

For today's children, the choice of food is almost limitless. Food from all parts of the world is available, and thanks to the modern techniques of refrigeration and 'freeze drying', can be good, if not totally fresh to eat. Supermarket shelves are crammed with an ever-increasing diversity of foodstuffs. Choosing something to suit even the most finicky eater has never been easier. Many foods are also especially designed to be easy and quick to prepare. A boon for busy people. Even a small town like Bingham boasts a variety of 'takeaway' food outlets - Indian, Chinese, Italian. In addition, children eat out at restaurants fairly often, go on foreign holidays, and so experience a far wider variety of food than would have been available in earlier times.

Manwai Yeung's mother makes a mouth-watering selection of Chinese and oriental food. Manwai says she likes to eat: *'Just whatever is nice. I like fish actually, but it has to be cooked nicely'*. They eat a lot of rice at home, but Manwai confesses to a liking for potatoes - not chips, which she says are too 'oily', but for school dinners she often has a jacket potato with beans or pasta.

Ben Selby and Laura Ball also choose fish as a favourite dish.

Not all children ate as well as others, especially during the war years. George Singleton's mother probably had a struggle to feed all the mouths at her table. George says that he always had porridge for breakfast, and that his mother was a good cook and would: *'sooner do without herself than let us go without.'* They used to have potatoes and vegetables, and the meat was often rabbit, which could be bought for about ten pence in the 1930s and '40s.

George's idea of a real treat was to go to Mr South's house, about two doors from where he lived and *'buy a pound of tomatoes and take them, eat them as you were going down the street. Sooner have tomatoes than sweets.'*

It is not possible to talk about children without mentioning sweets. They would have known where all the sweet shops were, and reminisce happily about aniseed balls, coconut slices and liquorice drops. Many of them also did quite a bit of the family shopping, so they would be familiar with all the local shops.

Dot Mabbott says there were lots of little shops. Hardstaff & Brown were the biggest shop. Millers on the corner of Newgate street made lovely pork pies, cakes, pastries and bread. The bakehouse was underneath the living room.

Hardstaff and Brown

25

She remembers pork pies and sausages wrapped up in greaseproof paper, put on pantry shelves. Sausages hung up from the shelves on hooks. There were no refrigerators in those days, of course.

Tommy Snowden sold practically everything: fruit, fish, vegetables, chickens, furniture, bric-a-brac. Mr Bell sold second-hand furniture. Lane's was a 'do-it-yourself' shop, and also sold paraffin. It had this motto 'All Roads lead to Lanes'.

Burgess's was a sweet shop, then Mrs Green had it as a wool shop. There was a shoe shop which Len Slater had later as a bicycle shop.

Where the travel shop in the Market Square is now, there was a haberdashery run by Miss Richardson, then by her niece, Miss Blunt.

Mr Harwood had a hairdressing salon with shaves at a penny a time. The front of the shop was a stationers, and also sold newspapers.

The two Miss Marriotts, Gertie and Ethel, ran the telephone exchange. Then there was White's the grocers, later to become Marsden's.

In Church Street was Doncaster's hat shop. Across the road was Doncaster's big shop, selling dresses, coats, shoes, lino, mats. Nearly everybody went to Doncasters for their clothes.

Dot has a truly remarkable memory, and what she hasn't told us, George Singleton has.

He remembers Seaton's the chemist in Market Street, the Co-op little shop, Kirk's butchers shop, the clinic where they would get orange juice and cod liver oil free, Mr Snowden's fruit shop, Mr Hart's butchers, and Cooper's, the plumbers.

Doncaster's

He remembers a Mr Miller's grocery, sweet and cigarette shop at the bottom end of Church Street. In the market place, Mr Gray's paint and wallpaper shop, and then the Crown Inn. Around the corner another pub (probably the old 'Bell' - since demolished), then Mrs Morris's sweet and cigarette shop.

At the bottom of Station Street was the old mill. At the top of market place was Hardstaff & Brown's bread shop, with the baker just around the corner. Mr Martin had the bakehouse.

Sally Wattam's memories are more romantic. She remembers Jimmy Skinner's, which she describes as:

'An old old-fashioned greengrocer's shop and it was very dark inside. He had a bow window, and when you went in, there was an old wooden counter, and he had a barrel of vinegar on the counter. It was very dark, but quaint.'

Hardstaff and Brown's she thought was *'quite a beautiful shop.'* She tells of mahogany counters, and *'on a shelf at the back were jars of tea, and they would weigh out dried fruit like currants and sultanas.'*

In Mrs Griffin's shop, near the church, you could get loose tea, and she says *'you got a nice smell when you walked in'*.

John Morris also remembers Hardstaff and Brown's as a shop of lovely smells. *'Ground coffee and smoked bacon.'* John mourns the passing of all those rich smells. He also remembers to this day, the smell of his Aunt's grandmother's famous lemon buns, and is cheered to think that he may be the one person left who knows the recipe for the buns, which he says, *'were a treat in all of Bingham'*.

Until the arrival on the scene of the phenomena known as 'teenagers', people mainly dressed for two reasons. To keep warm and to keep decent.

Young girls in the early 1900s were wearing vests, petticoats, skirts just covering the knee, combinations and bloomers. They wore ordinary stockings, sometimes knitted. No warm tights in those days In Kathleen

Selby's case, her mother got so tired of her falling down and making holes in the knees of her stockings, that she vowed, *'I'll buy you **socks** now, I'm not knitting any more stockings.'* Kathleen also wore fleecy leggings, the sort that buttoned up. Her weekday bloomers were navy blue and fleecy-lined, but *'your knickers used to have lace on the bottom, tied with ribbon, for Sunday.'*

Very often their boots would be bought from Doncaster's, either laced or buttoned.

Several decades later, Doncaster's were still going strong, and Freda and Joyce Castledine, as they were then, had *'new ankle socks and shoes or something at the Easter time, that was it, 'cos we used to get them from Doncaster's.'*

Not everyone was so well pleased with Doncaster's, however. Dot Mabbott tells the story of her father-in-law, who had been wounded in the first World War, and as a result had one leg shorter than the other. For the wedding of his son to little Dorothy Squires, he ordered a 'made to measure' suit from Doncaster's. Unfortunately they *'made the trousers to fit the wrong leg.'* So they had to be sent back and a new pair made. *'I remember that about Doncaster's'*, said Dot.

Freda, Joyce and brother Trevor

Many of the girls wore pinafores or aprons, a practice that was still going strong when Margaret Smith was a girl:

'Had to wear an apron over my dress, so that I didn't get it dirty.'

Lottie and her dog

Boys at this time, wore extremely boring and uncomfortable clothes by today's standards. Short trousers, long socks and little boots. Chig Pacey says that people don't realise how little money there was about at that time:

'*Kids in school went with holes in their shoes, or certainly in their socks, and sometimes in their trousers.*'

Derek Groombridge also remembers how, when boots were wearing thin, more studs were put in, until '*the studs were coming through your socks.*'.

Chig thought that during the war the clothing ration was hard for girls to bear, and remembers that his sister used to have some of his Dad's clothing coupons. He also remembers the fifty-shilling tailors, and that the first suit with long trousers he ever had, was from Burton's.

George Singleton must have been a typical little boy, and not at all grateful to his Mum for trying to make him look smart.

'*I had a new suit. Five year old, and I said I wasn't wearing **that..** She says 'You will wear it', and she put me it on. 'Now you can go out and play'. I did. I went down into Mr Hart's field and jumped into a pond. Spoiled the suit.*'

His poor mother must have been horrified. She didn't let him off lightly, though, or as George puts it '*I knew what day it was when I got back home*'.

Robert Selby remembers Cottage Homes boys being all dressed the same in '*little woollen pullovers with striped collars.*' Hubert Marriott does not remember this, but he does remember being adequately dressed, and truly appreciative of it:

'*When you got a new jersey, you thought you were a millionaire.*'

George in his new suit

Robert as a boy, had a wonderfully wild imagination, which obviously fed on stories like that of 'Scott of the Antartic'. He was quite cross that his mother, a strict vegetarian, and strong believer in not killing animals for their fur, didn't have an old fur coat that he could dress up in, when out pulling his sledge.

'*My great love was Scott, Scott of the Antarctic, and in the winter times when the snow was on the ground, we used to build sledges. We all had a dog, everybody had a dog in those days and... All the poor dogs had to pull the sledge.*'

He did have some clothes of which he was very proud, however:

'*I had a proper lumber jacket. A real Canadian lumber jacket........I also had real Indian moccasins.*'

He has nothing to say of his ordinary, everyday clothes.

No special teenage clothes as such, would have been available to Freda Hayes, Joyce Simpson or Margaret Smith. They would have been expected to wear the same sort of clothes worn by grown-ups, but scaled down a bit. It may be because of this, that they have little to say about their clothes. Freda and Joyce remember that a woman who lived opposite their grandmother's farm used to make '*our nice little smocked dresses. We used to have one the same - with a silk ribbon in our hair.*'

They have nothing to say of teenage clothes, though Margaret remembers with affection her first handbag:

'*It was small and black - made of a velvety material. I can always remember that handbag.*'

Fashion at that time, had not really recovered from the 1940s 'New Look', so dresses would have been quite long, certainly covering the knees, and quite full. Skirts would have been slim-line, although 'dirndl' skirts became quite fashionable following the Queen's (Elizabeth II) visit to Canada. Wearing 'swagger' coats or 'duster' coats, teetering on 4 inch stilleto heels, and wearing hats and gloves - that was high fashion then. Great for the sophisticated woman, but hardly the thing for the young pre-pubescent, teenage girl.

Freda and Joyce

Most young girls, going to their first jobs, would wear just what they had worn to school. As soon as their very limited wages would allow, they might buy a 'pencil' skirt, with either a slit or a pleat at the back, and a crisp, white blouse. Possibly a twin-set, or maybe a button-through cardigan, which the daring few would wear back to front just in order to ring the changes. Money was still very tight, but women have always loved clothes, and although there was no special fashion for them, young women managed to look *nothing* like their mothers.

By the 1960s, even before the advent of rock and roll, teenagers began to use clothes in a different way. To make statements about themselves and the sort of people they thought themselves to be. First 'Teddy Boys', then 'Mods and Rockers', and later 'Hippies', then 'Punks', and at the end of the century, 'Goths'. These fashions were not followed slavishly by all teenagers, fortunately. Most preferred to wear modified versions of the current trends.

Punk Hairstyle

As a young child, Barry Stewart remembers: *'Short trousers, long socks up to my knees, tank tops, no sleeve jumpers.'* From his teenage days, *''Ben Sherman' shirts with round collars, stay-press trousers and 'Crombies',* (a kind of overcoat) *big platform boots and shoulder length hair.'* From hers, Lindsay Smith recalls with affection, 'flares', zippy jackets, fleeces, Chinese dresses with big splits up. *'All sorts of funny things really, but they're all coming back in the shops now, so they couldn't have been that bad.'*

Lindsay Smith

From about the same age group, Jane Harding remembers mini skirts and hot pants, *'lots of long hair and beads.'* Maxi dresses and maxi coats, knee high boots, *'bright yellow lace up shoes that had red toe caps.'* Platform heels, bell-bottoms and flares. Lots of blue eye-shadow, lipstick and mascara. Two of her favourite shops were 'C&A' and 'Chelsea Girl'.

Carol Haynes and Jane Harding

The mini skirt was one fashion that 'caught on' in a big way with women of all ages. Even women who should have known better, took to wearing their skirts well above their knees. On the young and shapely, they looked sensational, and caused many a male driver's attention to be distracted, sometimes with serious consequences.

Karen Douglass tells us that she was a 'Goth' for about six months: *'Used to wear long black skirts. Everything was black.'*

She describes her make-up, saying that you were meant to make yourself look ill. The foundation was white, with really dark eye make-up and black lipstick. One of her friends used to dye her hair every week, and back comb it until it looked a total mess. Unfortunately she went too far, and eventually her mother had to take her to the hairdresser to have all colour stripped out, after it turned bright orange.

For a while, there was much emphasis on designer labels, and children were ridiculed at school if, for example, they were not wearing the 'right' sort of trainers. Happily that phase is passing, and our children of the late twentieth century show a healthy, pragmatic attitude to clothes.

Peter Ball: *'It doesn't really bother me, the designer label thing. I mean if there's something I like and it's ten pounds rather than thirty pounds, I know which one I'd rather choose.'*

Laura Ball

All of the girls interviewed from this period, like jeans and little tops, and wear trainers on their feet.

Laura Ball: *'I like to be quite fashionable. I wear different clothes every day. I like my trainers because they are nice and comfortable. I like to wear dresses, skirts, trousers and shorts as well, so I'm not that 'picky' with what I wear.'*

Joanna Hart: *'I like to be in fashion...jeans...tee shirts...I've got a denim jacket that I wear a lot.'*

Amy Balchin: *'Jeans, I like jeans all the time, and usually like comfortable jumpers and short-sleeved tops, and things like that. Trainers and that sort of thing.'*

For discos, they might vary it with a skirt or boots and certainly with make-up and hair nicely done.

The clothes girls wear these days are fashionable certainly, but also comfortable and appropriate. The attitude is summed up by Manwai Yeung: *'I like to wear just whatever is in fashion that I like. Anything that I think looks good on me.'*

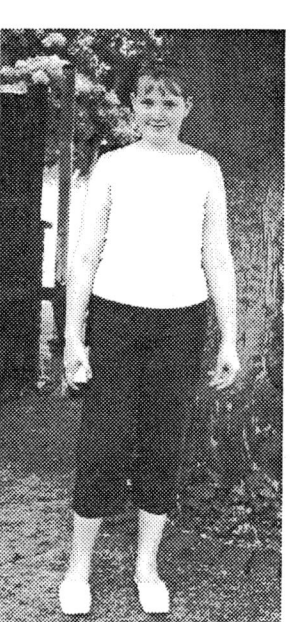

Amy Balchin

Given that there are often strong feelings against school uniform, it is remarkable how many of our children were, and are, content with the Toot Hill uniform. True, some of them couldn't wait to get it off when they got home. Either to get into every-day clothes to go out to play, or in Ben Selby's case, to go to work on his father's small holding.

Whether it was black and white and grey, or bottle green and cream, it seems to have satisfied most. Sally Wattam didn't like the green knickers worn for PE, but later, the addition of a little green pleated skirt, made them very acceptable to Lindsay Smith. Lindsay also found the uniform skirts very adaptable:

Manwai Yeung

'I had a grey skirt which went down to my ankles, and then for the following year, mum cut it down so that it was above my knee, because it was the style then...So we got quite good use out of the uniforms.'

The female of the species has always had a flair for fashion, and will probably always take an interest in the way clothes look.

Joanna Hart

Men also, from time to time have played the peacock. Even during the twentieth century, when most of the male population seemed to dress in drab uniform of one kind or another, there have been occasional bursts of sartorial experimentation.

It would be good to think that the twenty-first century will see a blossoming of masculine fashion. It is probably a forlorn hope that military uniforms will no longer be needed, but the unimaginative uniform suits worn by businessmen *could* finally become defunct.

School uniform serves a different purpose and provided it gives a degree of versatility, may be considered an acceptable necessity.

Gordon House

John Morris's Cottage

Children on Fairfield Street

Chapter III – School Life

Being the seat of the Rural District Council, Bingham didn't do too badly for schools at the turn of the century, having two main schools, the Wesleyan School and the Church School, as well as one or two little private schools run by well-intentioned ladies.

Wesleyan School now a private house

The Wesleyan School at the bottom of Kirk Hill closed in 1909 when the County, or Council School opened on School Lane.

The private schools faded away over the years with the emergence of more modern educational facilities.

Dot Mabbott: *'When I was four I went to a private school…up Miller's Yard, off Church Street. There were only about twelve of us and when Miss Horton's mother took ill she had to finish the school and I went down to the Church School.'* There is a notation in the Church school logbook, dated 23ʳᵈ June 1924: *'Admitted four children from a private school (Miss Horton's).'*

Kathleen Selby remembers *'there was the private school at the top of the Market, I think she took them from three to five that lady, and they all ended up at the Church School afterwards.'*

County School – now the Infants'

Until 1923 both the County and the Church schools took children from the age of five, the County School up to the ages of seven or eight when they moved up to the Church School – *'where we did our schooling until we were fourteen and then we left, fully-educated, supposedly,'* said Chig Pacey.

A re-organisation of the two schools took place in 1923 and the County School became the Infants (standards 1 and 2 only) and the Church School became the Senior Mixed (standards 3-7).

This system remained constant until 1953 when Toot Hill Secondary Modern School was built on land east of Mill Hill – a fine, modern school with three classrooms and a main hall for assemblies and extra-curricular lessons. This school took in pupils from outlying villages as well as Bingham and a great rivalry developed between Radcliffe and Bingham children. As Vida Smith recalls, *'Bingham and Radcliffe hated each other always. Radcliffe always beat Bingham at everything…Radcliffe lads always seemed a bit arrogant, I can always remember if it was snowing it was always them that put snowballs down your neck, so nobody liked them.'*

East Street showing Church School

By 1965 the population of Bingham was approaching 4000 and the number of children on the Church School register increased rapidly. Three annexes were in use, the Tithe Barn at the Rectory and two classrooms in huts on Mill Hill near Toot Hill School.

Robert Selby: *'Across the road from Toot Hill was a strange place, it was where the Land Army girls used to work from during the war. All the ones who were a bit slow in learning used to go there.'*

Sally Wattam *'went to the Tithe Barn because the Church School was so overcrowded and it was quite nice because it looked out on to orchards and it was a very old-fashioned room with two black stoves.'*

A new Junior School was urgently needed and Robert Miles Junior School opened on 3rd May 1965 in the grounds of the Rectory – the Rectory itself being demolished to make way for the bright new buildings, the latest in school development.

Many Bingham people deplored the destruction of such a fine house but the land was given free to the District Council by the Church to build a new Church School. The County Council, who funded the school itself, decided otherwise.

The old Church School was used as an annex for a year by Robert Miles and was finally closed in 1966.

Further development took place at Toot Hill in 1967 when large-scale extensions turned it into a Comprehensive School, enhanced two years later by the completion of the country's first joint use Sports and Leisure Centre,

Original Toot Hill School buildings

opened in April 1969 by Dennis Howell the Minister for Sport.

A second Primary school, Carnarvon, taking children aged from five to eleven, was built on Nursery Road at the eastern boundary of Bingham in 1968. The excavations for the foundations revealed many relics and artefacts from a mediaeval burial ground – the fact that Crow Close, the adjoining field was, and still is, a protected area didn't seem to deter the authorities from giving permission for a school to be built there.

At that time further housing development to the east of Bingham was expected, but to date, that hasn't occurred. In spite of that, Carnarvon School, together with all the other schools in Bingham, is bursting at the seams. We now have the situation of children being bussed in from other areas and Bingham children being taken to outlying villages because the Bingham schools are full.

Since the late 1970s or early '80s another category of child education has materialised – nursery schools, pre-schools and playgroups. Bingham today has at least four, and probably more, of these establishments, each 'conforming to all Social Service and Ofsted requirements', offering 'a friendly, educationally-stimulating environment' with 'professionally qualified staff'. Now the Government is planning to make nursery schools available to all four-year-olds.

Having provided better facilities and teaching methods over the years are adults these days demanding too much too soon of children?

The first twenty years of the century are too early for first-hand accounts so we had to resort to the school logbooks. At that time Harry Pilling was headmaster of the Council school and remained so until December 31st 1922. His wife Nancy, was a teacher. Mary Cowling, aged 94, remembers *'old Mrs. Pilling was my first teacher and we used to have to fetch her from her house down Kirk Hill. She couldn't walk so we used to fetch her.'*

Mr and Mrs Pilling with school group

Charles Pitt Hunkin was headmaster of the Church School, doubling up as Rate Collector and Registrar of births and deaths.

Both the moral and the physical welfare of the children seem to have been well catered-for according to the standards of the day.

Religion was a prominent, one could say dominant, part of school life, with frequent visits by the 'Reverend', regular testing, an annual report on religious instruction and closures for Feast Days and confirmations. Also recorded are frequent visits by the Nurse for head inspections, doctor's medical examinations, dental inspections, eye inspections, HMI teaching standards inspections, sanitary inspections and so on.

In spite of that some of the following extracts, written in clear, concise handwriting, depict the appalling conditions which were standard for that period:

30th June 1902 – 'School closed for one week for Coronation celebrations.' (Edward VII and Queen Alexandra).

HMI Report, Oct. 30th – 'This a capital school…the work is praiseworthy and the tone excellent.'

HMI Report, Mar. 1st 1904 – 'We found most of the offices for both boys and girls in a very dirty and offensive condition…and in view of the fact that the pail system is in use special care should be taken to ensure perfect cleanliness and sanitation.'

Feb. 6th 1905 – 'School re-opened a month late due to epidemic of measles.'

There are many absences recorded due to colds, influenza, mumps, measles, whooping cough, ringworm, chicken pox, diphtheria and other diseases.

Discipline and standards tightened considerably with the appointment of a new headmaster on 7th September 1908 – Edward Philip Day, who was to remain in office until October 1941. From his first week he applied new rules of behaviour and dress. Punishment was swift and severe:

14th Sep. – 'Gave notice of new rule, children to bring notes from parents explaining any absences from school.'

16th Sep. – 'Thomas Reuben Hart, aged 12 years, proved very obstinate this afternoon and was punished by one stroke on the left hand, three on the back and three on the buttocks.'

25th Sep. – 'Punished William Kettle, aged 12 years, for using foul language in the playground.'

Oct. 4th – 'A travelling entertainer gave an exhibition of paper and cardboard folding and modelling to the children at the end of the afternoon's session.'

Oct. 21st – 'Had to complain about the untidy manner in which some children were dressed.'

Oct. 22nd – 'Noticed a great improvement in the children's clothing.'

Nov. 9th – 'Robert Hart and George Butterworth are to lose their recreation this week as punishment for carrying on an indecent conversation.'

Feb.1st 1909 – 'Received a complaint about Albert Cowdell's stealing sixpence. Recovered fourpence and suitably chastised the boy.'

Mar. 3rd – 'Attendance affected by heavy fall of snow.'

Sep. 22nd – 'Visit from police to interview boys who had been trespassing after fallen fruit. Two of these boys have been punished at school before for a similar offence.'

Nov. 9th – 'Alban Cowdell expelled for a few days until his clothes have been cleansed. Today, the smell coming from them was too offensive for him to remain in class.'

Nov. 23rd – 'Mr S Blood has complained today of Miss Hemstock striking his son on the head thus bringing his head into violent contact with the desk and causing his gums to bleed. The teacher has been severely reprimanded.'

So the entries go on.

Punishments altered considerably over the century. In the early years Mr Day and Miss Adelaide Wortley, who joined the school in 1911, are remembered with mixed emotions. Dot Mabbott remembers 'Peggy' Day as being strict but fair, a very good teacher, someone she got on with.

George Singleton: *'Mr Peggy Day, he were a very good teacher. I used to get sixpence very often from Mr Day for mental arithmetic, I'm still pretty good at it now, at eighty three.'* He also adds, *'He and Miss Wortley, the teachers, used to have a cane, rap your fingers when you were doing something wrong, but if you did something really bad, he used to put you across the desk. Some used to put a pad in their trousers when they were going to have the cane.'*

Hubert Marriott: *'Mr. Day were very, very strict. I once just spilt a drop of ink on my school book and he used to have a stick…and he used to hit you across your hand with that.'*

Dot Mabbott: *'Miss Wortley was very strict. I just dropped a pair of scissors one day during the lesson* (needlework) *and I had to stand on the seat at the back until the lesson had finished. We only had a certain amount of things and you had to look after them. So scissors couldn't be dropped because you spoiled the points you see.'* Freda Hayes added, *'She used to throw chalk and rulers and all sorts of things at you if you spoke…or were not listening.'*

Robert Selby remembers her with deep affection and respect as a historian who *'enthralled with her teaching…mainly the Roman era she was interested in…a lot of us who were interested in her subject found them wonderful.'* But he also says she *'was very strict, she wouldn't stand any nonsense. She used to crack you with a cane, not particularly hard, but enough to know.'* Another teacher he recalls, Mrs Musson, *'used to crack your knuckles whether you'd done anything wrong or not…just in case.'* This teacher is indelibly stamped on Derrick's mind also, *'Very strict, she had one of the sit-up bikes and she'd ride through the Market Place and you near enough saluted her.'*

Another teacher mentioned by Lottie Castledine was Nellie Taylor. *'I used to be left-handed and she used to have a little ruler in her hand and would tap me on the knuckles and I had to put my pen in the other hand.'*

Another form of discipline, probably a result of wartime food restrictions, was experienced by Margaret Smith at the Infant School. *'Yes, we used to get shut in the classroom. There was one particular year I didn't want to eat my school dinner and I was locked in a classroom and made to stay there, alone, until I'd eaten everything.'* This experience was shared by Vida Smith: *'I can remember, in the Infant's School, this plate of food in front of me, and I just couldn't eat it, and I sat there the whole of the dinner time with this food and pudding, which I wasn't allowed to touch, in front of me.'*

As the century advanced so punishments moderated both in style and frequency.

Mr Middlemiss, headmaster of the Church School for eleven years and subsequently of Robert Miles Junior School until 1984, described his policy. There was a cane in school but it was only used in severe cases. He was the only one who could administer physical punishment, always with another teacher, and if possible a parent present. Often a talk to the parents was sufficient deterrent. John Morris was, and still is, a great admirer of Brian Middlemiss, *'He wasn't terribly strict but he instilled discipline in a rather nice way. I think it was more his voice, his authority, than anything.'*

From the comments of our younger interviewees we can follow the steady decline of physical punishment.

Lindsay Smith: *'There used to be the cane for girls and boys…when they had done something a few times, yes.'*

Barry Stewart: *'Mr Jarvis...would throw pieces of chalk...if he hadn't got your attention, there was the odd time a blackboard rubber used to come across. I can remember the ruler across the hand but I can't say I remember the cane.'*

Both Karen Douglass and Ben Selby remember a teacher at Robert Miles poking them with a pencil if they got something wrong. But Ben excused her, *'I think she had to stop doing that shortly after us...she was a really old lady and was probably stuck in her ways.'*

Amy Balchin: *'If you talked a lot or didn't get on with your work you got a detention, which meant you had to stay in at break or lunch, and if you did something really bad you got a Head's detention which was after school for about two hours.'*

Manwai Yeung: *'Well they gave you detentions and then a bad referral sometimes, which you had to take home and give to your parents to sign and give it back, and sometimes you get suspended if you are really that bad.'*

Joanna Hart: *'They had disciplinary referrals for a detention which you had to take home for your parents to sign.'*

Laura Ball: *'If you did something really wrong he could really shout, but he was like a friend really because you could talk to him about anything.'*

The policy of Robert Miles School today is vastly different to that of years ago. Behaviour of the pupils is exemplary because they are taught to have high ideals and they respond positively. Minor breaches in good behaviour are dealt with immediately with a verbal reprimand. Zero tolerance over small offences results in mutual respect and trust within clearly defined rules.

The Church School, built in 1846 only had two classrooms. Until 1923 seven standards of children had to be educated in those two rooms.

Lottie recalls, *'There were little desks and little chairs and there was just two rooms, the smaller one the Infants', you started there, then...the other room, the rest of your time you were there.'*

Dot Mabbott: *'There was no shortage of pencils or pens, pens with inkwells we had, in the desks for two mostly, in Miss Wortley's class. The next class I went into was the big room, that was one long room, standard 5 at one end...standards 6 and 7 at the other end. The heating we had was big coal stoves with a guard in front, but it still wasn't warm.'*

The Church School in 2000, now Church House

Robert Selby: *'It was a strange little school because it had only one room with a curtain going across, so if you sat near the curtain you were usually more intent on listening to what they were saying behind the curtain than you were on your own teacher. It had cast iron stoves and in the winter, because it was such a cold place we used to huddle round the stove and it took you all your time to stay awake.'* (The open fire stoves remained until 11th February 1957 when two Esso stoves were fitted.)

Vida Smith: *'At the time the big room just had a green curtain dividing it but a bit later on it did have a wooden partition, but you could still hear what went on between the two classrooms.'*

The Council school was more modern, having three separate classrooms and a hall. Freda Hayes: *'Yes, the little school had three classrooms. Miss Taylor was the first one you went to, she was an elderly lady.*

Miss Cooper, she was a Bingham lady and Miss Sides, the head teacher...she was very nice.' George Singleton remembers the blackboard and chalk and the big sandpit.

Derrick Groombridge: *'We always assembled in the hall in the morning and then you would go to your classrooms. You learnt to tie your shoelaces on a piece of stick and if it kept coming undone they'd stand you in the corner.'*

Jane Harding was in Miss Taylor's class, *'It was very much the 3 Rs, but I can remember lots of painting activities and sticking cereal boxes together...and nature walks, we'd go down to the Church to see the crocuses and collect sticky buds and things like that.'*

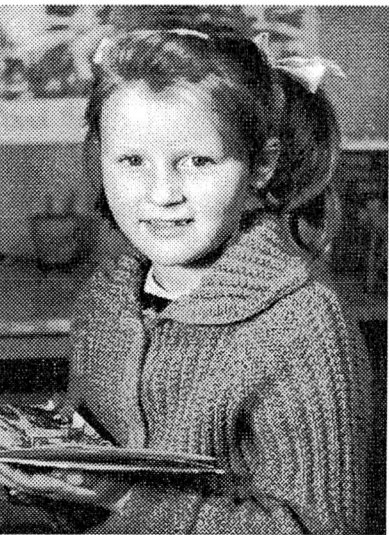

Teaching methods then were different to today's, as today's will probably be unlike tomorrow's.

John Morris: *'It was all blackboards, there was no computers or anything like that. It was all blackboards and notes and essays. We had a lot of textbooks.'*

Barry Stewart: *'We used to all sit in rows, you had your own desk and it all used to be off the blackboard, or your encyclopaedias or text books and that. Not like nowadays where the kids can key into a computer and there's three or four pages there for 'em. And they haven't even had to look for it.'*

Jane in the Infants' School

Jane: *'I can remember first of all having Mr. Jarvis who seemed very trendy at the time and he used to get us to learn our times tables by running up and down the classroom and the first one that got there had to shout out the right answer.'*

Play Hour in the Infants' School 1948

School logbooks reveal more about the conditions in school. Lack of time precludes using both schools' logbooks but the entries are very similar, so all the following information comes from the Church School, starting with the early 1920s. The results of Mr Day's insistence on high standards of behaviour, dress and work are evident. The Attendance Officer's weekly reports rarely mentioned truancy; most absences were due to illness or bad weather. Dental, medical and 'head' examinations still took place, but unhappily, illness and disease were still rife.

E.P.Day with Scout Group

Mr 'Peggy' Day (no one seems to know how he got the nick-name) was a strict disciplinarian but he was also a considerate and enlightened headmaster. It was not all doom and gloom.

A full week's attendance by a class was rewarded with a 'treat' – they were allowed to leave fifteen minutes early each day the following week. And, in winter months the afternoon lessons started and finished earlier to allow children from outlying districts to reach their homes in daylight.

Absences to attend Wesleyan or Methodist functions, including outings and tea parties, were condoned, as were absences for agricultural work – two days' holiday for potato picking was recorded.

Cricket and football matches against East Bridgford, Cropwell Bishop and Whatton took place, with Bingham usually the winners. So practice for these sports must have been regular.

There were two-day holidays for Goose Fair, also days off for Royal weddings, General elections, religious Feast Days, a week at Whitsuntide as well as the normal Summer, Easter and Christmas holidays.

The National Anthem was sung on Empire Day, and two minutes silence observed on Armistice Day.

The following are random entries taken from the logbooks:

27th Oct. 1922 – 'Coughing has made teaching in the Main Room a matter of some difficulty this week.'

18th Dec. – '39 absent due to measles.'

21st Feb. 1923 – 'Heavy snow fell during the night – 30 pupils absent.'

19th Mar. – 'Photographs taken of Class Groups during recreation interval this morning.'

'Peggy' Day and Adelaide Wortley with group of schoolchildren

9th April 1923 – 'Bingham Church of England Upper Standards School. **Main Room** – Standards 6-7 (44 pupils) taught by E P Day, headmaster. Standard 5 (28 pupils) taught by Miss Kathleen Jackson. **Classroom** – Standards 3-4 (57 pupils) taught by Miss A L Wortley.

The first week's work under the new conditions has shown that the majority of the children transferred from the Bingham Council School are backward in their work and some of them are distinctly uncouth in their manner.'

15th Jun. – 'Stafford Castledine was smoking a cigarette in the boys' playground during the dinner interval. This boy has been suitably punished.' (So not everything changed).

24th Sept. – 'A slate surface has now been fixed to the wall in the urinal in the boys' playground.'

20th Jun. 1924 – 'Five boys absent for varying periods setting potatoes (in mid-June!!)'

11th Jul. – 'Received a hand sewing machine (Singer) for school use.' (A representative visited the school on the 21st to demonstrate its use).

29th Jul. 1924 – 'Reginald Mabbott, head monitor, a boy in a thousand, left school.' (This was the childhood sweetheart and subsequently the husband of one of our interviewees, Dot Mabbott).

15th Oct. – 'Joseph Marriott cut open his head in the playground at 1.20pm and was sent for medical attention. As he did not return until 3pm he was marked absent.'

22nd Oct. 1925 – 'School caps are being introduced, probably for the first time in the history of the school. The girls have been supplied with theirs today.'

29th Oct. – 'The boys have been supplied with their school caps today.'

1st Dec. 1929 – letter to the Reverend H R M Hutt from A Tibbits, School Medical Officer.

'Dear Sir,

> I am pleased to inform you that on Nov. 5th the school nurse examined the heads of 47 girls and 52 boys at the Bingham Church School and that the total number examined were found to be absolutely free from any verminous contamination. This is a matter for gratification and I trust will be a stimulus which will help your school maintain a record of absolute cleanliness.'

23rd Mar. 1926 – 'Received a list of gramophone records which may be borrowed from Shire Hall to assist teachers in Musical Appreciation for senior scholars.'

31st May – 'Roderick Collins of Mundella School arrived here today for holiday teaching practice.' (He was to become headmaster of the Church School in 1946).

Electricity was installed on 8th September 1930.

6th Apr. 1937 – 'During the Easter holiday a four valve electric wireless set has been installed in the Main Room and a loudspeaker in the Classroom.'

27th April – 'Received from Messrs J Fry and Sons six dozen Coronation Beakers.'

11th May – 'Closed for three days for the Coronation of George VI and Queen Elizabeth, followed by Whit week. Each child on the books was presented with a souvenir Coronation Beaker supplied by the LEA.'

10th Jun. – Report on Instruction in Needlework – 'The Needlework of this school continues to maintain its interesting character…the garments show a real knowledge of construction, good taste and a varied interpretation which eliminates monotony and repetition.'

30th Aug. 1937 – 'Two minutes silence observed in school, the Service broadcast from the Cenotaph.'

Display of Needlework – Dot Mabbott front left

1st Mar. 1938 – 'Mrs Nora Musson (nee Bishop) uncertified teacher, commenced duty today.'

30th Mar. – 'Paid wireless licence – ten shillings.'

28th Nov. – 'The girls attending the Local Domestic Science Centre were given a demonstration of 'Electrical Washing' by a representative of the Hot Point Electrical Appliance Co Ltd.'

22nd Jun. 1939 – 'Heard broadcast of landing at Southampton of George VI and Queen Elizabeth after visit to Canada.'

29th Jan. 1940 – 'Heavy fall of snow, 24 absent.'

4th Nov. 1941 – 'Samuel Eric Dougan installed as headmaster.'

But only until July 1946 when Roderick Collins took over.

Roderick Collins with school Group

Suddenly the style and content of the logbook changed. As well as recording normal school procedure there are regular mentions of sporting events and cultural and social outings. A school Swimming Club was formed and 30 boys and girls taken to Victoria swimming baths after school. Later a class was taken swimming to Highfields Lido. A coach for football was appointed. School Sports Days and Inter-school Sports took place.

There were visits to Clifton Colliery, the local Gas Works, and the Trades Exhibition.

25th June 1948 – 'Seventy five children over eleven were taken by train to London King's Cross, then transferred to motor coaches for a tour of the city, the Houses of Parliament, Westminster Abbey, The Tower and London Zoo.'

On 17th June 1949 there was a trip to Liverpool by special bus, which also involved a ferry trip and the overhead railway. Two weeks later there was a visit to Southwell Minster to compare the architecture with that of Liverpool Cathedral.

Drama became significant and school concerts and Carol Services performed.

Parties were taken to see films, Henry V, Nicholas Nickleby, Hamlet, also the opera The Barber of Seville at the Theatre Royal.

An HMI Report of 20th June 1952 illustrates the change both in outlook and ambitions of Bingham's children after the Second World War. No longer was agriculture accepted as the obvious employment, a widening education had produced a thirst for better things – and more money. The Report said: 'Some pupils are transferred at eleven to Grammar, Technical and Art Schools in West Bridgford and Nottingham. Of leavers at fifteen, very few take up agricultural work, boys find employment in distributive and other trades or in factories in Nottingham, and the girls, for lack of local light industry, in factories there also.'

It added, 'The Headmaster is a graduate with an enlightened outlook and a quiet purposefulness.'

Brian Middlemiss succeeded Roderick Collins as headmaster of the Church School in 1953 when the latter moved up to Toot Hill Secondary Modern School.

It was in the second half of the 1960s that three new schools, Robert Miles Junior, Toot Hill Comprehensive and Carnarvon Primary were built using the CLASP system (Consortium of Local Authorities Special Programme). They were the latest in school development with a large multi-use hall surrounded by blocks of 'teaching areas'. Mr

Carnarvon Primary School in year 2000

Charlton, first headmaster of Carnarvon described his school as 'one of the first open plan schools in the country.' Together with the new school designs came new equipment and teaching methods. Out went individual desks and blackboards, in came chairs and tables and green marker boards (supposedly kinder to the eyes). Mr Charlton explained the methods used in his school – 'We tried to extend each child to its full potential'. There was no strict timetable but every child had reading, writing and numbers practice each day. Those who were able could get on with their work so that the teacher could concentrate more time with the slower ones. The 'times tables' were discarded and emphasis was put on using numbers more freely.

Sports such as football, cricket and swimming were encouraged, but not in a competitive way. This was to ensure that all children got the same attention, not just a few who excelled in a particular field.

On the other hand, Mr Middlemiss, headmaster of Robert Miles, was more a traditionalist. He relished the fact that his school was in all the football and netball leagues in the Newark area. Although a more relaxed attitude to teaching methods was adopted, it did not go so far as abandoning all the old ways. Some of his staff were particularly remembered for their discipline.

School 'Outings' during this period are worth mentioning. 'We could charter a special train,' Mr Middlemiss said, 'sometimes shared with another Boys' Secondary School,

Robert Miles Junior School in year 2000

probably nine or ten coaches, and go to Skegness or Cleethorpes, one time we went to London'. That trip ended rather chaotically. There was a threatened train strike, due to start at midnight. Although ensuring in advance that it would not affect them, the train stopped at Leicester on the way back and would go no further. Double-decker buses were sent from Nottingham to fetch the schoolchildren but the adults from the train aggressively commandeered them. Fortunately, (having fewer Health and Safety rules and regulations in those days) everybody was crammed on somehow, sitting in the aisles, on the stairs and on each other's laps.

Coach trips to Derbyshire, Whitby, Hornsea, Kingston upon Hull, which involved a coach, train and ferry ride, and other venues were organised from Robert Miles. Mr Charlton also mentioned educational visits to Boggle Hole at Robin Hood's Bay where countless fossils could be found.

Life in the playground hasn't altered all that much over the years. Some childhood games are timeless, some seasonal and others fashion fads.

Mary Cowling, aged 94 mentions football and skipping. Margaret Smith adds hopscotch, chase and whip and top to the list. Vida Smith refers to marbles. Also Ben Selby, *'never knew any rules but we played it.'* Dot Mabbott tells how *'the boys had the playground at the back and the girls' playground at the front wasn't very big…so we used to play in the street outside, East Street, and we used to have skipping and jumping and ball games, but we had to mind peoples' windows.'*

George *' used to like football, and cricket…conkers, when it came to conker time.'*

Chig Pacey: *'The games varied, it used to go in cycles. When the horse chestnuts were about it was all conkers, or whip and top. And what they called wild bulls or something, where you jump on somebody's back and everybody got knocked over. Quite rough they were.'*

Sally Whattam played *'hide and seek, netball, snobs, whip and top, hopscotch, skipping, ball games.'*

Jane Harding: *'Skipping games… we used to play French skipping with elastic – two friends would stand opposite each other with a ring of elastic round their legs and you'd stand in the middle and jump on the elastic and have to follow various patterns.'*

Derrick Groombridge: *'When we were at the Infants' we used to have football and we'd draw the goalposts on the wall. And in winter we would make slides from one end of the school top to the other and it would get busier and busier. They never put salt on it.'*

Lindsay Smith: 'We used to play hopscotch and jump at Robert Miles and we used to have things, I can't remember what they were called, where you used to clang them together but they were stopped doing those because they were doing people damage, hurting people's wrists, so they banned them from school'. [NOTE: these 'clackers' were two wooden balls on strings which, when manipulated vigorously, would bang together above and below the hand - theoretically! They caused a lot of bruised knuckles and cracked wrists – also mentioned by Barry Stewart].

Karen Douglass described with exuberance, *'One of the games was you put a ball in a sock and stand against a wall, hitting the ball against the wall sideways and up over your head and down between your legs and the sock would stretch, so you used to tie it up again and it would eventually break and you'd get another.'*

Manwai Yeung describes a game played a generation earlier by Jane: *'Skipping, with those elastic things where two people stand either side.'*

Joanna Hart: *'We had a lot of clapping games and skipping and hopscotch, or I used to play football with the boys with, like, a tennis ball.'*

Laura Ball: *'Skipping, tig, kiss-chase, and 'duck duck goose', that was a good game, a lot of us liked to play that. Well, there's a big circle in the middle of the playground, everyone stands round it with their arm out and someone comes round the circle and taps them on the arm and they have to run round the circle until they catch them.'*

One of the joys of childhood has always been the carefree involvement with others in playground games like tig, skipping, hopscotch, ball games, conkers and so on. The designers of Toot Hill Comprehensive School, in their wisdom, did not incorporate a playground. Architecture in the 1960s was innovative and, in some cases, disastrous. Maybe the idea at the time was that children over the age of eleven were too sophisticated to play anymore. There are wonderful facilities for sport, but that is a different concept. There seems to be a lack of joy, vitality and exuberance in the following comments:

Barry Stewart: *'We didn't really have playground games like you do at Junior and Infant school…we used to congregate under a little archway where you had a tennis ball and you'd start off with two on either side and by the time the dinner hour was finished there was like ten on each side.'*

Peter Ball: '*We mainly just wandered around school. In the summer we played football...just a kick around, or sat up on the field, but in the winter there was nothing to do really.*'

Amy Balchin: '*There wasn't a playground, there was a field so you could go up there in summer, but there were loads of places we could stay, inside.*'

Joanna Hart: '*We just sort of walk around with our friends, talking. I sometimes go to the library.*'

Laura Ball: '*Usually I'll go up to the cafeteria to have my lunch and then we usually sit in the houseroom and listen to music really, and talk.*'

What prospects were open to our 'children' once they had left school? For the first part of the century most girls were expected to stay at home and help with housework or farmwork, or look after younger children or older relatives. Lottie left school at thirteen, having obtained a Leaving Certificate, to help her mother at home on Starnhill Farm. Mary Cowling said, '*I didn't go anywhere, I had to stay at home...my mother got invalid and I had to look after her.*' Kathleen Selby also stayed at home due to delicate health.

Dot Mabbott's parents must have been more progressive because when she left school she went to Binn's Business College to learn office work. But when she married and a baby was on the way she left work to look after her family.

It was different for boys. They were expected to start work straight away – according to their status in life. George excelled at arithmetic but became a farm labourer because at that time poor children were not given the opportunity to pursue further education. Hubert was transferred at the age of twelve to another Boys' Home in Basford and after two years was 'picked' by a farmer to work on his farm. He joined the army in 1939.

Chig Pacey on the other hand, joined Shipsides in Nottingham as a garage apprentice when he left school at fourteen. This was the career chosen by Barry Stewart a generation later.

The wartime years opened a lot of opportunities for women to work in different occupations, but office and shop work were still the main stand-byes. Margaret, Freda, Vida, Sally and Lindsay all opted for one or the other in spite of having yearnings for something different.

Vida Smith: '*No, you just left school at fifteen and, this is the big difference between then and now, there was never any question of you not going to work for whatever reason, because there was a job and you took it.*'

Sally: '*There wasn't really a lot of choice, it was either going into a factory or working in a shop or office.*'

It was in the late 1960s or early '70s that careers advisors emerged and colleges and universities became more accessible to everybody, not just the intellectually elite. Ambitions blossomed.

John Morris always knew that he would follow his parents into the family business so he went to Nottingham University and Clarendon College to get his City and Guilds and Hygiene Certificate for catering.

Jane took A and O levels and went on to do her nursing training at Nottingham General Hospital.

Karen took CSEs and left school at sixteen to go to college for two years to obtain her Preliminary Certificate in Social Care.

Peter is taking 'A' levels and hoping to go to university to do teacher training.

Amy wants to be a lawyer.

Laura typifies the adventurous spirit of today's youth: '*I've got a lot of ambitions actually, I want to travel round the world, I want to swim in the Olympics...I would like to be a Sports Science teacher.*'

From this small survey we can see how the conditions, expectations and ambitions of children and their families have changed over the century. At the beginning everyone 'knew their place' and those at the bottom of the scale were not expected to better themselves. Thankfully attitudes and circumstances have changed and all children should be given the same chance to succeed. This is the case in a relatively affluent place like Bingham, but isn't necessarily true in some other areas. Bingham children are the lucky ones.

Now, at the beginning of the Twenty First Century Bingham has four excellent schools, catering for children from the ages of five to eighteen. All of them have reputations for high standards in academic, social and sporting activities.

Robert Miles Junior School is one of the top junior schools in the country. It has achieved Beacon School status. The HMI Report of March 2000 has awarded the top mark of **excellent** in all aspects of teaching and strategic use of resources. Standards in English, mathematics and science are well above the national average. The pupils are articulate, well-motivated and take great pride in their school. There is a full range of teams - cricket, football and netball in the Newark and District Leagues; a chess club which enters inter-school competitions, and after school activities covering sports, chess, cycling proficiency, a choir and summer games. There are also in-school competitions for Spoken English, Science and Technology, and Handwriting.

School equipment includes computers, with an internal network, video recorders, TVs, and OHPs. Calculators are allowed in certain circumstances, e.g. scientific calculations, otherwise brainwork is encouraged.

We can see how extensive the changes in all aspects of school life have been throughout the Twentieth Century. One of the most important factors is that children are now treated as a valuable part of the community and their welfare and education are of paramount importance.The whole world is their oyster. They can travel physically by jet plane and mentally by Internet.

The future is an open book and who knows what will be written in it?

E P (Peggy) Day and class with young woman teacher

Starting Early - Story Time in the Bingham Libaray

Chapter IV - Recreation

The places children played, and the games they played during the century, were as many and varied as the children themselves. There are, however, a few common themes running through their stories.

The old favourites of cricket, football and tennis are mentioned by many. Rather more surprising, is that Dot Mabbott was amongst those who played cricket. In fact she was a member of a ladies cricket team. She also played badminton. Some of the girls mention netball and hockey, and many of the children speak of going swimming. There were the usual organised activities of Youth Clubs, Guides, Brownies, Cubs, and of course, Girls' Brigade and Boys' Brigade. Unsupervised,

Girls' Hockey Team

were the pastimes of sledging in the winter, and skating on local ponds, and wandering far and wide.. There was a thriving Boxing Club, and Chig Pacey was lucky enough to have a snooker table at home.

Many of the children remember 'pictures' (cinema) in the Women's Institute Hut on Station Street, where the seats were hard and when the film broke down, which it quite often did, there would be 'cat calls', and many little hands would make shadow pictures on the screen. Some of the films they remember seeing include: 'Calamity Jane', the 'Treasure of the Golden Condor', John Wayne in 'Stagecoach' and Roy Rogers in many films. Derrick Groombridge says that all the little boys used to sit in the front rows playing Cowboys and Indians, and as they got older, would dream of the time when they would be sitting on the back row with a girl. When 'Rock Around the Clock' came to Bingham, there were queues down the street. The man who ran the picture show would not stand for any nonsense, however. As Derrick says, *'He'd come and clip you around the ear, and out you'd go.'*

Sally Wattam remembers that he charged nine pence for children and one shilling and sixpence for grown-ups. John Morris thinks he used to pay two pence. Memory tends to be selective, and cannot be regarded as infallible.

Chig Pacey: *'If we wanted to go to the pictures we'd ask, but at the time, there was the new Rex at Radcliffe. That was only about threepence or fivepence.'*

George Singleton: *'We used to go to the Ritz picture house. Sixpence. Eightpence on the train, sixpence for the picture house, then we used to go into the Empire cafe for tea, which was about eightpence. Second house at the Empire up in the Gods, sixpence. That was half a crown for a weekend.'*

Well, almost.

There are also fond memories of black and white picture shows that Eric Green, a previous mayor of Bingham used to run. He would show films starring Charlie Chaplin and Laurel and Hardy. These were very popular with the children.

Another memory that several of the children have in common, is of the fair that used to come to Bingham market place two or three times a year.

Lottie Castledine: *'There used to be a little fair come every year in the market place. Just one or two swings and horses and a cake walk.'*

Dot Mabbott: *'We had a fair every year in the market place. Cakewalks and swings and horses.'*

Derrick Groombridge: *'Proper fair would come. Coconut shies, the lot. I mean it'd come regular. Every year there was a fair until about 1957. I think it died. I think it were dying out then.'*

Sally Wattam: *'I can remember going on the cake walk, but not a lot more about it.'*

They may have been quite sad when the fair no longer came to Bingham, but at least they had the Festival to look forward to.

The Festival, in one form or another, has been a time of celebration in Bingham for many years. At one time, it would have been held in the Rectory Gardens. Later, when the Rectory had been demolished and a school built in its place, the Festival was held in the grounds of the school. Nowadays, for the most part, it is held in the Market square. It lasts a full week, but the one special day is Fair Day, when there is a procession, and the Festival Princess is chosen. It is an opportunity for the people of Bingham and surrounding area to show how talented they

Bingham Festival in Robert Miles field

are. There are dancers, singers, acrobats and musicians of one kind and another. All the various organisations of the town have little stalls on the Market Place, with games to play, or produce to sell. It not only publicises those organisations, but allows them to make a little money.

Festival Princess under Buttercross

There is a game that may be peculiar to Bingham, that many of the children tell us they remember playing, called 'Hollow/Holler'?.

George Singleton: *'Well you used to get in gangs and play what they call, Housey, housey, follow, follow the leader. Hollow, Hollow, if you don't hollow, you won't follow.'*

Derrick Groombridge: *'We'll play hollow... We'll make the bounds the Market Square. And they'd pick the one that's that was on. So the one that was on, he'd got to catch you all.'*

One person would be nominated 'it' and the rest of the players would hide all around the village, within their set 'bounds'. They would keep calling 'holler', and the person nominated, would have to find them. Not an easy process, we are told, as there were many places to hide in the village in those days. As Derrick tells us, the person nominated would sometimes get tired of looking and go home, leaving the others still forlornly calling 'holler'. Children have a wonderful sense of fair play, so the next day, Derrick tells us, the one who left would be told:

'You're on tonight, kid - you left me [us] and we were still out. We got into trouble.'

Derrick was well respected in the village, being a member of the Boxing Club. He and his friend, John Pritchett, who was British Middleweight Champion, reached the Great Britain finals of the junior ABA championships:

Derrick: *'We were like stars in a little village. Everybody knew you. Now I can walk down the street - they don't know who I am.'*

Derrick Groombridge

John Pritchett's mother, Derrick tells us, was a hairdresser. *'I can remember going in his house one day, and I can remember playing with a toasting fork, and thinking this toasting fork, these two holes will line up with these two holes on the plug, and I shoved it down there and it's gone 'Bang'!..and I thought, Good grief, I wonder what's happened. I'd got my coat on. I said "John, are we going to play football", and we ran out of the house. Six o'clock, his mother's got a queue outside.'*

I wonder how long it was before the power came back on.

Derrick was doubtless a bit of a rascal when young, but with a genuine love of Bingham: *'It was a village, you've got to realise. It wasn't a town like it is today, and we would have fun all over. We would have real fun.'*

Another 'hollow' the children speak of, is a different thing altogether. Where Toot Hill school now stands, was a hollow in the ground - a hollow with steep banks. When it snowed, the children would, 'whizz' down these banks on their sledges. Chig Pacey had a sledge called 'Bluebird' of which he was very proud. He also remembers that some of the more adventurous boys used to sledge down the railway embankment on the Melton Mowbray line.

Derrick Groombridge: *'There was a great big hole in the top of the fields - top of Toot Hill...a great big hole in the ground that sledging was absolutely marvellous in...Some people got super sledges, some people got not very good sledges, and on one side it was dead rough, and they'd take you, they'd say, 'I dare you go down there'. But on the other side it were like a sheer drop...this side it were sloping it were like sloping down, so we could spend many a time up in the hollow, playing in the winter...'cos it was so marvellous just to have a hole in the ground, that you could just be in and sledging...not hit anything and there were nobody in the field. Just like that and hours and hours.'*

Even sledging down the steep but relatively safe banks of the 'hollow' could be dangerous. Freda Hayes tells us how they were sledging with other children, one of whom was an evacuee: *'We used to lay on the sledge, about four of us, and he was on the bottom because he was the big boy, and we came off and he knocked himself and cut his tongue, and it was awful.'*

He had to be taken home to his surrogate Mum and the doctor. That gave them all a terrible fright, but Robert Selby tells us of a far worse disaster he had heard of: *'One of the lads got killed on the railway line. He came down on this sledge and then struck his head on the lines.'*

George Singleton played football for Bingham, but remembers having to be in bed for 8 o'clock at night. He and his friends would play tricks on people. The Town Crier at the time, was nicknamed 'Froggie': *'When we were lads, he'd chase you. We used to go and take his gate off. And we'd bodge it up.....and we used to yell 'Froggie', and his door opened and he'd come out yelling 'I'll Froggie you'...as he come down he'd touch the gate - the gate had gone!'*

George says that there were garden fetes all over Bingham, with choirs of Bingham people, piano players, jugglers and with comedians Sam Blood, publican, and Mr Brown, of Hardstaff and Brown.

He says his father was something of a comedian too, or at least a practical joker. He used to try to frighten a friend of the family, by dressing up in a white sheet, and standing in the garden when she would come home late. *'Didn't frighten her though'*, says George, *'The only thing that frightened her was when he put his wooden leg in the bed she used to sleep in. That stopped her coming in late'.*

Sally Wattam used to play in a friend's house or garden at 'shops': *'This girl's mother would let us get everything out of the pantry and put on the table, and we would weigh all the groceries on scales.'*

Another friend lived in a shop on Market Street. *'It was a greengrocer's shop, and at the back of their house was a fish pond, and we used to go and play around this fish pond and have picnics round there....Also, we used to play on the banana boxes.'*

In the summer holidays, she would visit her friends at Mr Knight's farm, and play on the haystacks and ride on the haycarts.

Some of the children spoke of listening to the radio or 'wireless'. Dot Mabbott says that they had an old 'Crystal Set' wireless with earphones. There was always a bit of a scramble as to who got the earphones first. Many of the children remember when television first came into their homes. At first only in black and white, then later in colour. Many of them remembered 'Blue Peter', a children's programme that is still going strong. Sally Wattam also remembers 'Muffin the Mule' on television, and hearing an announcement on the radio when she was six, that Princess Elizabeth had given birth to Prince Charles.

Besides the old 'Crystal Set', Dot remembers songs around the piano and card games at Christmas time. At Sunday school, they had a 'star' card. *'And it was how many stars you had on your card, you got the appropriate book at prize giving time.'* There would be a Methodist church concert every year, performed by the 'Young Leaguers'. Mrs Horace Shepperson used to write the words and Mr Giles Doncaster, the music. Occasionally they would be taken on Sunday school outings in a lorry, with seats down the sides and a tarpaulin over the top.

Lottie Castledine's enjoyments were very quiet: *'On a Sunday night, when it was nice..... we used to have a little walk right round the fields as far as the Smite... Then my Dad would read us a little bit out of the Bible, and then we'd go to bed.'*

She spent a lot of time with her lambs. They followed her everywhere, and she tied little bells around their necks with ribbon.

Her parents only went out on a Saturday night: *'And that's when they went to the Vaults pub in Bingham. When we was*

Lottie with her pet lamb

younger, me Dad had a pony and trap, you see. We used to come in that, but when we was old enough, we all got bikes then, and on a Saturday night we used to come down... We used to stay with Granny and Grandad on the Banks, while they used to go with them, and they'd go to the Vaults for a drink, Dad and Mother. They didn't stay late you know, and then we used to come back home.'

Then, when she was about seventeen or eighteen, she would come into Bingham to stay with a friend, and she and the friend would go to a dance in the 'coffee rooms' which were next door to the 'Wheatsheaf'. She would stay overnight with the friend, then go back home after church the following day.

There being so many orchards and allotments in Bingham, it is only natural that a lot of 'scrumping' went on. Vida Smith certainly remembers her brothers climbing out of the bedroom window in order to go scrumping in Mr Roweth's orchard. She also remembers getting caught red-handed, sitting in a field full of garden peas:

'Sat munching, popping peas and eating them.'

The farmer, accompanied by his dog, marched the terrified children into the village square, the children expecting to be hauled into the police station. Instead, he just left them there, saying not another word. I expect the children spent a few uncomfortable weeks, thereafter, waiting for the policeman's knock on the door.

Derrick Groombridge had a nasty moment in Waplington's orchard. This orchard was obviously a regular port of call for the lads, but this time they got a nasty shock: *'We thought 'good grief', there's a bloke in a chair. Must be a ghost...He's sat in a rocking chair, this Waplington. Just a real old gentleman wi' a beard..and he really, really looked very weird in an orchard. And we all ran out of this orchard and thought - we're not going there again.* Derrick says *'whether I was a scoundrel or what, I don't know, but I did have some fun in the village.'*

Margaret Smith had a very busy and exciting childhood. Her father was trainer for the football team, and her home was used as a changing room for the team. She used to go to away matches with the team, in a lorry with a covered back. Weather must have been a problem in those days. She remembers snowdrifts so high, buses only went as far as the bottom of Saxondale hill.

Freda and Joyce played anywhere and everywhere in the fields. The cricket field, Parsons Hill, the wash-pit over the railway, up Mill Hill into the woods, and up and down the railway banks.

Later they learned country, ballroom and old time dancing, and also used to go to an occasional square dance. They remember playing table tennis at the Youth Club in Fisher Lane, and also playing records on an old wind-up gramophone. They also used to go to dances in the coffee rooms.

Children crossing railway lines – Bingham Station

Coffee Rooms – rear view

On May Day, there were little concerts and Maypole dancing in the Rectory. One particular year, Freda was 'Queen of the Flowers'. She had a long white dress covered with flowers. The other children were dressed as flowers, and she had to sing and bring all the flower children on to do their dance.

Robert Selby, our 'inventor', who was always thinking up exciting ideas, which sometimes worked: '*We made a canoe out of laths, and this was..an Indian type canoe, and we'd found a piece of old tarpaulin..and we were on this pond and it kept sinking.*'

How did Robert overcome this little set-back? '*It was near the gasworks and out of the corner of the gasworks they used to pour a lot of tar. So we went down there one day, and we coated the whole of this canoe with tar. And it sailed perfectly. It was wonderful, it didn't leak. But we were completely covered in tar. Clothes, face and hands.*'

His Dad had to use 'thinners' in order to remove the tar, but as Robert says, '*It left us a bit sun-tanned*'.

There used to be a very fine wrought iron bridge over the railway line. Barry Stewart remembers rocking it from side to side, but that is surely not why it is no longer there: '*When the old steam trains used to come through, used to run, and I'm sure you got on top of the bridge before the old steam train come under. But we used to get two or three of us, and you used to stand in the middle of it, and you used to rock it from side to side.*'

Barry seems to have had a fascination with the railway. He remembers the old waiting room on the Grantham side of the line: '*A great big old waiting room with a little fire, coal fire at the top end and a great big wooden bench all the way right down one side, and you used to spend like, the cold nights in there.*' It also, is there no longer.

Freda – Flower Girl

One especially exciting memory he has, was of coming out of Sunday school and running all the way to the top of Tythby Hill in order to watch the army bomb disposal squad blow up an unsafe bridge on the Melton Mowbray railway line.

A different kind of adventure was experienced by Karen Douglass. Karen used to go to a club called the 'Elm Tree':

'It wasn't a disco, but it had a bar in it, but it was more like a club that stopped open to about 1 o'clock in the morning.'

She says it was near the river Trent, and that:

'I can remember them being really good times. Actually, they were brilliant.'

Some of her favourite singers and pop groups were; 'Spandau Ballet', 'Duran Duran' and Paul Young. She could buy half a pint of lager for 45p and a vodka and coke for 70p.

Several children in these later years, speak of drinking alcohol. Peter Ball also says that although he does not think that hard drugs are used in Bingham, nevertheless there is quite widespread use of marijuana. He thinks that it might even have reached children as young as eleven.

Many children over the century have succumbed to the dubious pleasure of smoking cigarettes. Not Ben Selby, although many of his contemporaries would have done. Children still have not realised the folly of smoking, and still hide around the back of the leisure centre in order to avoid being caught. Apart from cigarettes, Ben thinks that cider would have been the hardest 'drug' children would have encountered in his young day. But he was very much the outdoor type, and when not working on his father's allotment, would have been away across the fields with his fishing rod or his air rifle. He and his friends would build tree houses and dens, and make bows and arrows. He remembers there being a lot of building work going on in Bingham at that time, and that he spent lots of time watching the builders at work.

Rather like his uncle, Robert Selby, he was always ready for experiment and adventure: *'I once tried to build a catapult and catapult my friend across the flats on Carnarvon Place. '*

But it was the river Trent that satisfied his liking for adventure:

'I were about ten or eleven, we all used to ride up there on our bikes with a tractor tyre inner tube round us and jump in.'

In contrast to Ben's leisure time activities, leisure time for children at the latter end of the century, seems very tame. Apart from taking the dog for walks and going shopping in town, most of their outside leisure activities are organised sports. Most of them spend their free time watching television, playing on their computers, listening to pop music or talking to their friends. They have friends to stay at their houses often, or stay over at their friends' houses. Pop groups and pop stars they mention include 'Hearsay', 'Westlife', Craig David and Robbie Williams. Television programmes some of the children have remembered watching are: 'Bonanza', 'Tom and Jerry', 'Blue Peter', 'Top of the Pops', 'Deputy Dog', 'Black and White Minstrels' and 'Tinga and Tucker'.

Amy Balchin feels that there should be more things in Bingham for young people to do. For instance, she thinks there should be a Cyber Cafe, or a Skating Park. Peter Ball says that a few rowdy people at the Leisure Centre get thrown out and spoil it for the rest: *'I know for a fact that when I was thirteen or fourteen, I used to go up to the Leisure Centre, and if I was seen in the Leisure Centre by someone who worked there, and it happened to be a Friday night, then they were asking me what I was doing, why I was there. And that was because there was a small few that used to go and mess around, and it spoiled it for everybody else.'*

The children all agree that charges at the Leisure Centre are too high, so that while it is a good facility to have, it is too expensive for them to use often. Peter Ball again: *'It's no wonder that the kids are hanging around on street corners. Nottingham is too far to be able to go when you're that young at night time..And there's nowhere else to go apart from Nottingham. There's nothing to do in Bingham.'*

Bingham Leisure Centre~,

The Banks, Bingham, Notts NG13 8
Tel No: 01949 839638
Fax No: 01949 875295

FITNESS AND FUN FOR EVERYONE

- Two Swimming Pools and Grass Screen slide.
- FITZY's fitness suite
- Eight lane athletics track
- Two floodlit artificial turf pitches
- Snooker room
- Four multi-purpose halls
- Three squash courts
- Eight tennis courts
- Lounge bar and cafeteria
- Grass pitches

If it's Aerobics or Archery, Badminton or Basketball, Sub Aqua or Socialising you name it, there's something here for you
Whatever your age!!

Leisure Centre

They do have outings to zoos or amusement parks, like Alton Towers or the American Adventure Park, and most of them go abroad for their holidays, but the Bingham they inhabit, is a quite different place from that described by older people.

One of the saddest stories that show how much Bingham has lost, comes from Robert Selby's memory of a 'Fairy Dell'. The 'Fairy Dell', was a place that the children of Bingham thought of as either haunted or enchanted. It was near the Fosse Way and had a natural spring,

Robert: *'It was a lovely peaceable place, and water just used to bubble up out of it and there used to be lots of wonderful plants including slipper orchids.'*

The children would camp there in homemade tents. Roman soldiers were reputed to have been seen there, and groups of ragged people. Whether that is true or not, there *were* trees and rare plants there. Those early children certainly knew how to use their imagination rather than mind bending drugs in order to see the enchantment in a place.

Special occasions, like holidays, birthdays and Christmas, are the high points of most children's lives. At Christmas, Sally Wattam would hang up a bolster, not a stocking. Presents she remembers getting include paint-boxes, snakes and ladders, a toy stove, similar to an 'Aga', on which pans of water could be heated with the help of a 'night light'. She had Enid Blyton books, Girl and School Friend annuals, and Film Review books, but her favourite present was a Pinocchio doll, which she still has.

In her stocking, Dot Mabbott would have *'a bright new penny, an orange, some nuts and a small toy.'* Each Christmas, Harold Kirk, who was the son of the author James Prior Kirk, would come to stay. Besides Sunday school outings, she remembers outings on the train to Mablethorpe and Skegness.

Chig Pacey remembers going to Sutton on Sea every year, before the war: *'Sutton on Sea. Great! Lovely sands, digging holes and having donkey rides. Last time we went was '38, 1939, with the war looming. We never went, never since then have I really gone on holidays much. I sort of lost the 'yen' for it, so to say.'*

At Christmastime, Mary Cowling's father would always insist that there be thirteen around the table for Christmas dinner: *'Mother used to have us all home at Christmas, and Dad would always sit thirteen at the table. I mean when Margaret was a tiny baby and she used to have to sit in a chair. Because if there was more than thirteen, she couldn't sit at the table.'*

Kathleen Selby is one of the few that recall going to Goose Fair in Nottingham. But then she went quite often, and would get a 'cockerel on a stick', which, I gather, was made of rock. One year when she was unable to go, her father bought her a special 'Goose Fair' present. This was a kitchen set, probably quite like the oven set that Sally Wattam had for Christmas. Unbeknown to her mother, she used to cut a potato up very small, and cook it in a little dripping. Another special present was one made by the boys at the school where her uncle, who was the Head teacher, also taught woodwork. It was a doll's house.

Kathleen: *'And it was papered with real red brick paper, especially for it. It had chimneys, it had stairs, it had little fireplaces. We'd even got a little bit of red paper in the fireplace that looked like a fire. And there were beds for the upstairs, and he'd made a settee which somebody had stuffed with cotton wool. And there were little chairs and he'd got a table.'*

A quite special present.

Every year they had a holiday at Sutton on Sea, Mablethorpe or Bridlington.

Ben Selby remembers having an Action Man and a bike for Christmas. He spent a lot of time riding up Belvoir hills on the bike. He used to get taken to Rufford Park or the seaside for a Bank Holiday treat.

Margaret Smith went to her grandmother's house for Christmas. They had a real old fashioned Christmas, with a sing-song around the piano, played by her grandmother. Her grandfather played the cornet. She remembers Sunday school trips and having to recite or sing a song. The Chapel would be full to the brim - a special day.

Christmas is Laura Ball's favourite time of the year: *'I love Christmas; it's my favourite time of year. We have big dinners and I love Christmas morning. That's my favourite. I get quite a few presents actually, from family, friends, Mum and Dad, Santa.'* Her special memory is of first learning to ride her bike, helped by brother, Peter.

Joanna Hart also loves Christmas. To her it means the Christmas tree, hanging up stockings, having Grandma to stay and turkey dinner. She enjoys parties with the family and discos with her school friends. Sometimes she has joint disco parties with a friend, in Bingham Pavilion. Holidays are taken abroad. Her favourite holiday place is Cyprus.

Manwai Yeung's Christmas dinner is rather different. Her mother prepares a buffet style meal, with many little Chinese delicacies. They do have a Christmas tree, but would be more likely to go to a friend's house and have a 'karaoke' evening, than slump in front of the television, or play games. Manwai says that although her mother *'doesn't really feel comfortable going to a foreign country'*, they nevertheless, went around Europe, visiting about seven countries in a very short time.

For the Chinese New Year, again her mother makes lots of Chinese food. The children have 'pockets' into which the grown-ups put money, and of course, the whole of Bingham is treated to a firework spectacular.

Every Christmas, Freda and Joyce would have in their stockings, a few sweets, an orange, *'a doll if you were lucky'*, a jigsaw and a book. Mr Shepperson, a leather saddler, would make them either a little handbag or a purse. But the most exciting day of the year for Freda and Joyce was Boxing Day, when the 'hunt' would meet in the Market Square. All their relations came on that day and their grandmother would make all the cakes and mince pies: *'And they all came for a cup of coffee, and they were all coming in and out all day.'*

The Hunt - Meeting in the Market Square

Having watched the hunt leave, the children would, *'get packed out with a bottle and sandwiches, because we used to traipse the whole fields, to try to find out where they were going, and we used to follow them, and we used to be gone nearly all day following the hounds.'* So they would spend the whole day trying to follow the hounds and the huntsmen in their bright, scarlet jackets, mounted on their strong, magnificent horses. What a wonderful sight it must have been. Strange that so much magnificence should be concentrated into chasing a little fox.

John Morris's Christmases were certainly full of laughter and conviviality. The fact that his parents were working up until the very last minute in their butcher shop, did not detract one bit from their enjoyment. As John says:

'Christmas time's a time for families and home.'

He says that he can still remember his Uncle Tom sitting in a corner, singing 'Red, Red Robin', and sliding under the end of the table. *'That was a Christmas party to remember.'*

A story of John's, is one that his Dad told him. There is something very special about those rare occasions when your Dad takes the time to tell stories of his youth and I think that made this a special memory for John. This particular night, John's Dad was in an expansive mood, having come in from the White Lion, and began telling him stories about farmer Brown's threshing engine and Frank Derry. Then he told him this story:

'They came down from Derry's Lane to the Wheatsheaf pub for a pint of beer every night, and this particular night they all said 'goodnight' to Frank....They said 'goodnight' to Frank at nine o'clock, and quarter to ten Frank walked in the pub ready to start his night out. He didn't realise he'd been in before...He'd walked halfway home and the wind was blowing. He'd turned round to light his pipe against the wind, and started smoking and walked back to the pub.'

Children at play in Union Street – 1940s

Punch and Judy Show – Robert Miles Field

Chapter V - The War Years

During the Twentieth Century two successive generations of Bingham's children experienced a period of time during which England was at war with Germany. Few of the people we interviewed for this project were old enough to remember the Great War of 1914-1918 – ironically called the 'War to end all Wars'.

Zeppelin

Ninety four-year-old Lottie Castledine, born at Starnhill Farm, recalls one little nugget relating to WW1 though, *'One night my dad heard the zeppelin going over, he fetched us out and he'd got the stable lamp and held it up for us to have a look. We saw it go over, it came quite low, and we watched till it got out of sight. It made like a humming noise.'*

This is born out by entries in the Parish Records:

'On Monday January 31st 1916 at 6.20pm a zeppelin flew quite low directly over the Church in a westerly direction. At 8.30pm another flew over the town also in a westerly direction. One was noticed flying to the south and the other to the north. At 9.40pm one returned flying eastwards and at 12.45am February 1st another flew eastwards directly over the town. No bombs were dropped and no damage done to the immediate district. Towns in the counties of Derbyshire, Leicestershire and Staffordshire suffered heavily – total number killed 60, injured 101. Had the zeppelins arrived 24 hours earlier they would have found the Church brilliantly lit and full of people. Under the circumstances evensong was abandoned for the time being and held at 3.30pm, as it was felt sure that the Germans would, on the first favourable opportunity, repeat this dastardly work of warfare.' Signed HRM Hutt.

Sunday March 5th – 'A zeppelin flew to the east of Bingham. A star-shell was dropped on Gooden's farm, adjoining the Starnhill, in the Parish of Whatton one and a half miles away. A bomb was dropped at Shelton burying itself in a ploughed field. No damage was done in the district. The zeppelin came over in a snowstorm.'

Not a great deal can be gleaned from the Bingham Rural District Council meetings of the time. There is a mention in September 1914 of 'accommodation and catering provision for recruits now responding to the national call to arms'. Also several enquiries during the following months from the Local Government Board as to the availability of hospital accommodation for the use of the War Office in cases of enteric fever and other infectious diseases. But anything to do with the war seemed to take second place to more pressing local business like appointing an Inspector of Nuisances and dealing with sanitary clearance.

But the schools' logbooks are more revealing – both in describing the heart-warming efforts of the children and teachers to help the war effort, and also the stoical way life went on as normal.

No mention was made in either the Church school or the County school logbooks of the outbreak of war in August 1914.

In February 1915 both schools recorded the overnight billeting of soldiers, followed by having to clean and ventilate the rooms next morning.

Harry Daft aged 18 Lottie's brother

Furniture was damaged and the floors left in a filthy state. On a later occasion, a teacher's desk was broken into and several items stolen, including two pairs of scissors, a box of pen nibs, two dozen partly-used pencils and a packet of sewing needles – a great loss at the time.

The following entries in the logbooks tell more:

Church school 29th Mar. 1915 – 'The children subscribe ten shillings towards the UMCA Fund for 'Children's Huts for Soldiers'.' (Ten shillings was quite a lot of money in those days, but in today's decimal money it's fifty pence).

12th May 1915 – 'Thirty-six children are each giving one or more eggs weekly to local Red Cross collections for wounded soldiers.'

The following week the County school logbook also reports the egg-collecting 'for soldiers in France'. Tuesday was designated 'Egg Day'.

What turned out to be an amazing coincidence followed this. One must assume that the children put their names and addresses on the eggs they donated because two children received letters from wounded soldiers thanking them for the eggs. The teacher of the little girl who received the second letter recognised the name of the soldier as being a former pupil of the school. Correspondence was set up and he promised to visit the school when he recovered.

Church School 13th Sept. 1915 – 'Admitted six boys (two families from London). They have come to live in Bingham temporarily to escape the zeppelin raids.'

24th May 1916, (Empire Day) – 'The Church school children subscribed sixteen shillings to the Overseas Club's Fund to provide tobacco for our prisoners of war in Germany.'

The same day the County school children had a 'penny collection' to supply comforts (tobacco, chocolate, etc.) to 'our soldiers at The Front. Collected eight shillings and sixpence.'

There are repeated entries in the logbooks detailing monies collected in Savings Associations and other wartime charities.

A lot of emphasis was put on helping the war effort by juggling with the school holidays. The summer break was called 'Harvest Holidays'. A week was taken off it and moved to October for potato picking. Leniency was exercised over absence from school to help with farm work, though absence for any other reason was severely dealt with.

Lottie and her sister Elizabeth

One unusual entry in the Church School logbook worth mentioning – 20th November 1917 – 'The Ministry of Munitions sent for the eight hundredweight of horsechestnuts collected by the children of this school.' That's a lot of conkers!

On January 7th 1918 the Church School children were taken to cheer some of the first repatriated prisoners of war from Germany who were passing through Bingham.

On 13th September 1918 the children were told to gather blackberries for soldiers and they would be paid threepence a pound for them. But which soldiers received the blackberries was not recorded.

At last, the war ended and the Armistice was signed on the eleventh hour of the eleventh day of the eleventh month.

On November 12th a letter was read out in the Church School from Major General Boyd, Officer Commanding of the 46th North Midland Division to the Lord Lieutenant of the County:

'In the name of the Officers, NCOs and men of the 46th North Midland Division, I would be grateful if you would grant the boys and girls in your County a holiday in honour of the storming of the St Quentin Canal, near Bellenglise, on September 29th 1918 when the Hindenberg Line was broken and over 4000 prisoners and 70 guns taken; also in honour of the Battle of Ramicourt, three days later…breaking the Beaurevoir-Fonsomme Line…etc.'

Following the notation of this letter in the logbook was this addendum – 'It should be placed on record that seven men at least in this gallant Division attended this school in their younger days'.

In spite of the request the school was given a half-day holiday only.

And the County School didn't seem to know anything about it because the only mention in their log book was on November 15th – 'Mrs. Randall visited the school bringing the news that the Armistice had been signed. This caused much rejoicing both amongst the teachers and the children'. But no holiday!

In the 1930s the idea of another war within twenty years of the last conflict must have filled the minds of most people with horror. Particularly abhorrent was the thought that gas bombs could be, and possibly would be, used.

With the advent of radio, and blossoming television, news from Europe was immediately available and as it became more ominous preparations for defence were embarked upon all over the country.

This time, the local authorities in Bingham were not slow to follow suit. As early as April 1937 an Air Raid Precautions Committee was formed to consider the appointment of air raid wardens and the introduction of training in anti-gas measures. It was agreed that a pamphlet 'Protection of Foodstuffs against Gas' should be purchased and distributed to all food distributors and dealers – fifty copies at twopence each.

In June 1938 the Rural District was divided into zones and requirements were drawn up for wardens, first-aid parties, ambulances, decontamination centres, casualty and mortuary areas, etc., etc.

The committee authorised the purchase of 100 rattles at 3/- (three shillings) each, and 'whatever quantity is necessary of a similar rattle for women wardens' at a price of 2/4d (two shillings and four pence) each', 70 hand bells with webbing handles at 10/3d (ten shillings and three pence) each and up to 100 whistles 'of a similar type to a police whistle'. [NOTE: three shillings is equal to 15p in decimal money].

An Evacuation Committee was set up in January 1939 and its first tasks were to draw up a full list of surplus accommodation and appoint Billeting Officers.

On 1st May the Clerk to Bingham Rural District Council received a letter stating that 2,220 evacuees from Sheffield would be allocated to the District.

In June a Draft Evacuation Scheme was drawn up – the evacuees would arrive by three special trains on the same day; train 1 at 10.52am would carry 744 evacuees; train 2 at 2.09pm, 674; train 3 at 5.37pm, 767. The County School was to be the reception area.

Bingham itself was to take 221 evacuees and plans for the purchase of blankets and bedding, and the distribution of emergency food rations were formulated.

The foresightedness of all these preparations proved to be invaluable when war was finally and irrevocably declared on 3rd September 1939.

At the meeting of Bingham Rural District Council on 21st September the Chairman, Mr F Thorpe Perry so eloquently and dramatically proclaimed:

> 'Since the last occasion on which this Council met, the Sword which has dwelt uneasily
> in the scabbard has now been drawn and we are at war.'

He could have been a speech writer for Winston Churchill.

Evacuation from Sheffield went ahead; Food Control and Welfare Committees were set up; a further 250 pairs of blankets were purchased at 5/11d pair (five shillings and eleven pence - 29p in decimal money) and the Fire Brigade Committee agreed to purchase 100 stirrup pumps at 24/6d each. Two months later a much-needed Fire Station, complete with fire engine and trailer pump, was established behind the Council Offices.

In May 1941, still fearful of gas attacks, the Civil Defence Committee decided 'In consequence of the stress laid by the Minister of Home Security on the risk of gas by the enemy it is desirable that a Mortuary Superintendent, fully gas-trained, should be appointed'. Mr C Coleman was appointed and Morris's barn on Long Acre was earmarked for use in case of emergency. 50 fibreboard coffins had previously been purchased at 11/8d each (58p)

So how did the declaration of war affect Bingham's children? Chig Pacey recalls, *'Well I didn't really take a lot of notice of it but my father, he was in the First World War in the Navy, he wasn't very happy about it.'*

This was probably the consensus of children everywhere. Ignorance was bliss.

The first obvious effect was two extra weeks' summer holiday, which probably did not cause the children a great deal of distress. The Church School log book (18th September) noted 'Reopening of school two weeks late due to outbreak of war and evacuation of children from industrial areas. Admitted ten evacuees'.

Air Raid Precautions and gas mask (respirator) drills were carried out immediately and repeated regularly. All children had to carry their gas masks with them and woe betide a child who forgot to take it to school. Freda Hayes remembers going to school when she was five with her gas mask in a little box.

What the ARP drill entailed is not noted in the logs, but the construction of air raid shelters did not commence until October 1940.

Evacuees arriving at Bingham Station June 1940

Summer merged into winter and the dreaded onslaught did not materialise. This quiet time was known as the 'phoney war'. But it did not last long.

When the enemy occupied Northern France the English coastal towns were considered at risk and evacuees from Yarmouth were sent to the District. Chig Pacey remembers the evacuees, *'My mother and father were sort of concerned with billeting, I know at home we had three girls for a few weeks until they found placements for them.'*

The summer holidays of 1940 were not as child-friendly as the previous year, being reduced to only one week (Wartime Emergency) and lessons were split into morning or afternoon sessions due to overcrowding and staff shortages.

The Church School logbook 1937-1945 provides many interesting details of how the war affected the school and the lives of the children:

5th Oct. 1940 – 'Mr Horace Gray has fixed adhesive protection to school windows.' (This entailed putting a criss-cross pattern of sticky tape over the glass to prevent shattering during a bombing raid).

9th Oct. 1940 – 'The children used air raid shelters for the first time when anti-aircraft fire was heard in the immediate neighbourhood.' (Subsequent ARP drills saw the children 'safely under cover within two minutes').

Wings for Victory Week

April 1941 – 'The school admitted 32 evacuees, mostly from Littlehampton.' (The W.I. hall was brought into use as an emergency schoolroom for 28 girls with one of their own teachers).

9th May 1941 – 'After considerable enemy activity in this district last night attendance was seriously affected.'

27th May 1941 – 'Respirators worn for five minutes – length of time to be increased during coming months.'

15th July 1941 – 'Received from LEA 1 stirrup pump, 1 sand container, 1 bucket, 1 long-handled shovel and 1 long-handled rake.' (For dealing with incendiary bombs).

6th March 1942 – 'Military Authorities requisitioned the Domestic Science Centre as a cookhouse.'

July 1942 – '15 children absent due to agricultural employment.' (The older children helped with the harvest and potato picking due to farmworkers away in the Forces).

Apart from recording regular ARP and respirator drills and mentioning various Savings Weeks – Warship Week, Spitfire Week, etc., there were no significant entries until 1945.

Salvage Drive

9th May 1945 – 'School closed for National Holiday to celebrate VE Day.'

30th Nov. 1945 – 'Children weighed and measured for issue of supplementary clothing coupons.' (Those qualifying could get extra coupons).

20th Dec. 1945 – 'School closed for VJ Party.'

Home life for our 'children' was obviously also affected by the war. The District escaped most of the terrors of war because of its size and locality. But it was not isolated from the physical presence of wartime activity. There was a large influx of military personnel - an Army camp at Whatton, an RAF base at Newton, which was 'home' to a Polish squadron as well, and the Canadian Air Force flew from Langar airfield. There were Land Army girls and, after a while, German and Italian prisoners of war. Frequently, endless convoys of army vehicles, both English and American, passed through Bingham.

'The Americans used to throw gum out to us,' Freda Hayes remembers, *'it wasn't like our chewing gum, it was much nicer.'*

Robert Selby: *'My dad was in the Foresters going to Italy and they were going by convoy and we walked down to the Fosse but we never saw him. There were hundreds of vehicles, maybe thousands, going by.'*

The siren went off frequently, mostly at night. A searchlight battery was situated in Crow Field, its powerful beam picking out planes on their way to bomb Nottingham or Grantham.

Chig Pacey: *'We had a siren of course, apart from that it was a bell or a whistle, and a rattle for mustard gas. We never used that rattle. But I remember the bell and whistle.'*

He also remembers the blackout curtains going up and his father ordering the shelter to be dug at the bottom of the garden in the orchard. *'It was a proper job, deep concrete and brick walls, railway sleepers and all the surplus put on top, so we would have been quite safe. We never went in it. The nearest bomb was about a mile away. It sounded a lot closer but it was near Newton camp.'*

Freda Hayes: *'We had an air raid shelter in our garden, in the corner. We used to go in there and we always used to play in there, after the war. My uncle had a Post Office at Langar and a bomb dropped in his front garden. But it didn't go off.'*

Fortunately, not many bombs were dropped in the Bingham area.

Food rationing did not appear to cause many problems either. Being a rural community there was no shortage of fruit or vegetables. The butchers were well-supplied with locally killed meat.

Dot Mabbott: *'If you killed a pig during the war...you had Mr Miller, or Jack who helped him, come up and deal with the pig for you. He'd make you pork pies and sausages, wrapped up in greaseproof paper.'*

There was a plentiful supply of wild rabbits and game to augment the diet, and in those pre-myxomatosis days rabbit was an acceptable and enjoyable dish. But the main restraint to a wide diet was, as it will always be, affordability.

Kathleen Selby: *'Being vegetarian I had to sign a paper to say I wouldn't eat anything that wasn't on the ration, fish, game or rabbit, to get the cheese ration and nut ration. I could go to the Savoy Health Stores once a month and get a pound of shelled nuts.'*

Joyce Simpson: *'I can remember the dried eggs for omelettes, we used to love that.'*

Chig Pacey: *'Rationing? In some ways being in the country we were quite fortunate because my father was a farmer's son... he used to go shooting during the season and we got a lot of rabbits, hares, pheasants, partridges, ducks and pigeons which supplemented the rations. I think what affected us most, as children, was the sweet rationing.'*

Freda Hayes: *'We were lucky because we had the farm, you see, and Gran helped out such a lot and we didn't go short of much at all, just meats and hams, but being on a farm we always had rabbit pies. It was basic, plain food.'*

Joyce Simpson; *'I remember going on a Saturday morning and fetching the sweet ration with the ration books. Once they had gone that was it, you couldn't have any more till the next week. We only had sixpence, just enough to get a quarter of sweets and that was it.'*

Coal was rationed. As coal was the main source of heating and cooking, this could have proved to be a bit of a problem. But there again, Bingham had its own local Gas Works. Many of our interviewees recall taking carts or wheelbarrows to collect sacks of coke, still smoking hot, for sixpence or ninepence a bag. Freda Hayes also remembers going up Mill Hill to collect wood and logs and anything that would burn to keep the fires going.

But the resilience of children to accept most situations and different types of people is demonstrated by the following memories:

Robert Selby remembers the prisoners of war: *'We had a pillbox and air raid shelter at the bottom of the garden and the German and Italian prisoners of war were pulling them down. I was so interested in it they thought it was wonderful and they made me a shovel out of wood. They used to wear dungarees and black triangles on their sleeves. Well my mother made me some dungarees and one of them got two black triangles and gave them to my mother so that I could be like them. They were very kind you know.'* He also says, *'I used to get quite used to the sirens and things like that. We had some Canadian cousins who came to Langar and they used to spend a lot of time at our house. We used to listen to the radio and when Germans were killed I used to say good, but I was told off for that because I was told everybody is the same.'*

Chig Pacey used to *'lay in bed and instead of counting cars going past we used to count aeroplanes, which made a change. There was a lot of flying going on then from Langar and Newton.'*

Freda Hayes recalls sleeping under the big kitchen table at her Gran's house when the sirens went. Her sister Joyce says they had *'A Land Army girl come to live with us during the war 'cos my dad was away, she had a farm to go to, she just lodged with us and had her food, but she used to help mum a lot.'*

Sally Wattam: *'I was three during the war and I can remember sitting there on the cellar head with my mother, father and sister and my father used to fetch Mrs. Biddle, who lived at the fish and chip shop to sit on the cellar head because they were frightened that if a bomb dropped on the fish and chip shop it would go up in flames with all the fat they used.'*

Chig: *'Oh yes, there was ITMA and one programme I really liked was Variety Bandbox. Father used to listen to the news of course, religiously, and I do remember asking him what they put in the newspapers before the war started because the front page was all war news.'*

The storm clouds of war, which more often than not leave a trail of death and destruction in their wake, passed gently over Bingham. Of course, there were individual tragedies, some lost uncles, fathers or brothers; Robert Selby lost a great-uncle in the First World War and George Singleton lost his eldest brother in the Second, but for most of Bingham's children it seems to have been a time of adventure rather than sadness. It added a touch of spice, of excitement to their lives which peacetime Bingham lacked. It brought strange and exotic people into the area, Canadians, Germans, Italians, Poles, as well as cosmopolitan British servicemen and women. Timetables and routine were broken but life went on. It was the time when Bingham was woken out of its rural doze, the time which signalled change and expansion, the time which dragged Bingham well and truly into the Twentieth Century. A bit late, but better late than never.

Military Band in Market Square

Military Parade in Market Square

Chapter VI - Religion

Unsurprisingly, few of the children at the latter end of the century, have anything much to say about religion. The church has so far declined in power and influence, that most children of today would only ever considering entering a church for a wedding or a christening. Joanna does admit to getting on really well with her Religious Education teacher, and having chosen RE for one of her 'options'. But Religious Education in school these days, consists of learning a little about all the different religions of the world. At least this gives children some idea of the many religious organisations that they might decide to belong to in later life, and it seems a healthier attitude to the subject than that described by Lottie Castledine.

As Lottie got older, she used her own discretion, but she says:

'We went to Chapel in the first place - used to go to the Wesleyan Chapel, because Mr Hardstaff and Mr Brown were Wesleyan Chapel people.'

Lottie's father, you will remember, managed a farm for Hardstaff and Brown.

Once, when the weather vane cockerel was taken from the roof of the church to be re-gilded, the rector of the time had the school children jumping over it as it lay on the ground. When it was back in place, he said, they would be able to point up and tell people, 'I've jumped over that cockerel.'. The rector *may* have been Canon Hutt.

Canon Hutt, who was rector of Bingham from 1910 to 1933, was a rather stern man of the old school. His writings in the church burial registers are fascinating. He would add little comments, as when he describes the zeppelin that flew quite low over the church in a westerly direction at 6.20pm on the 31st January 1916. He goes on to describe further the events of that night, when 60 were killed and 101 injured, but not in the local area. The one thing that concerned him most, was that just 24 hours earlier, the church had been brightly lit and full. He doubtless felt that God had given a special dispensation to his little flock.

He writes of one poor soul who had died, '6'6" tall and built in proportion, but with the heart of a one year old.' Another entry describes the departed as having spent 40 years in the workhouse. And another tells of a man run over by his own wagon. He did not die immediately, but died later of septic poisoning. Yet another entry was for a Ricardo Cope, who was so well loved that when he died, there were 750 people at his funeral.

Even more fascinating and intriguing, are the entries in Canon Hutt's own special code, giving his own very

Church of St Mary & All Saints

personal thoughts about those who had 'passed on'. From some of the comments that can be read, I would expect some of these personal thoughts to be fairly frank, and him to be fairly stern with his assessment of us poor sinners. But he must have had a softer side.

Dot Mabbott tells us that he was the first of the rectors to open his garden to the people of Bingham.

Of the Rectory she says: *'It was a lovely old place'.*

And of the gardens:

'You could roam anywhere. In Canon Hutt's day, you could roam anywhere in the garden..It was a big roaming garden....He kept gardeners and chauffeurs and that sort of thing'.

The Old Rectory   photograph courtesy R Whittaker

This facility was appreciated by the children of Bingham, and later when Bishops Gelsthorpe and Lasbury came to Bingham in about 1953, they appreciated it even more.

At this time, children were allowed into the house as well as the gardens, and could play snooker on a full size table. Mrs Gelsthorpe also played a large part in the village, in organising a girls' club. She allowed the girls to pick up any fruit that had fallen, but they were not supposed to pick fruit from the trees.

Vida Smith: *'That's what we were told - can't say we stuck to it.'*

She tells of fetes in the gardens and dancing around the Maypole. Vida also appears to have changed her allegiance, because she went to Sunday school at the Primitive Methodist chapel, but then was in the church choir, when Bishop Gelsthorpe was in Bingham.

The bishops and their curate, Peter Lillingstone, also taught the children to play croquet and clock golf. They placed no restrictions on whereabouts in the gardens the children played, except for those imposed by the gardener. So if he was cutting the grass or pruning the roses in a particular area, the children were asked not to go there until he had finished.

Bishops Gelsthorpe and Lasbury

Dereick Groombridge: *'Two gentlemen were the bishops.'*

Derrick also tells us that if you wanted to be confirmed, and went to confirmation classes: *'They would have breakfast laid on for you.'*

Methodist Chapel

Peter Lillingstone started the Boxing Club in Bingham, and it has been an important part of village life ever since.

The current Rector is the Rev. David Harper.

Many of the children remember Sunday school outings, concerts and celebrations of one kind or another.

Lindsay Smith: *'Me and my brother used to go to Sunday school every Sunday morning...enjoyed Chapel because we had a social life with it...used to go on outings and sports days. Go to the seaside and Twycross zoo.'*

The current Methodist Church Minister is the Rev. John Hudson.

66

There is a Baptist Church who meet at the Robert Miles Infant School Community Hall, and whose Minister is the Rev. Lorraine Stanley.

The nearest Catholic Church is in Radcliffe on Trent where the Parish priest is the Rev. Fr. Anthony Franey.

After the established Church, the Methodist Church has probably had the most influence in Bingham over the century, and is still a force for good in the town.

Most of the children, whatever church they officially belonged to, managed to be included into the special occasions of all the churches, and in this way, the essential message seems to have got through.

John Morris: *'I was confirmed and I went to Sunday school, but I don't go to church now. But I don't think that makes you any worse a person for not going. I'm religious in my own way.'*

Chig Pacey: *'When I was young we never used to have to lock the doors. Everybody was honest.'*

Derrick Groombridge: *'A very moral society - you could walk in one another's houses...Nobody would pinch anything from anybody. '*

Canon Hutt with Choir

Independent Primitive Methodist chapel
Long Acre

Former Independent Primitive Methodist chapel
now the Horse & Plough Public House

Conclusion

'*It was a nice little village, where everyone knew everyone else and everyone knew what everyone else was doing.*'

Margaret Smith, describing the Bingham she knew as a child.

Margaret was a child of the 1940s, but she could just as easily have been describing the Bingham her mother, Mary Cowling, knew as a child, two or three decades earlier. Children from this early period of the twentieth century say their childhood was ideal, and paint a cosy picture of peace and tranquility - nothing but orchards and sheep and freedom to roam.

At the beginning of the project, this was the kind of idyllic environment we expected to encounter through the memories of our older interviewees. After all, they were young in the early part of the twentieth century before the advent of the motor car. Of necessity, people worked and shopped near to where they lived. There were no huge motorways cutting up the land, and families lived closer together for help and support. Peace and tranquility was a reality.

But the above remark also brings a sense of the claustrophobic aspect of village life, that was probably as true of Bingham, as it is of small communities anywhere.

Villagers most likely *did* know what everyone else was doing, and although some may have found this extremely irksome, it may have served the purpose of keeping the children safer than they might otherwise have been. Local people would have been well known to one another, and strangers would have been immediately identified, and probably watched very closely.

Certainly no one ever worried in those days, if the children wandered off over the fields; even if they were away for the whole day. On the contrary, parents would pack them off with a few sandwiches and a bottle of water and not expect to see them again until about tea time.

Change when it came, was sudden. The developers moved in, and new estates with a few hundred houses here and a few hundred houses there, began first to fill any open spaces in the centre of the town, and then to eat their way into the surrounding green fields.

Building developers in Bingham have been allowed to sprawl and smother all the land that was at one time orchards and fields. Swallowed up into new housing estates, are the 'play places' described by the children of the first half of the twentieth century.

The catalysts that enabled change to come about so quickly were the motor car, and to a lesser extent, the railway. People could move out into the countryside to live, and easily travel to their work in town. What they failed to realise was, that if enough people move to the country, then country *becomes* town. And that is exactly what happened to Bingham.

But for the most part, children today seem quite content. Their homes and surroundings are comfortable, and equipped with music centres, televisions and computer games to keep the whole family entertained and occupied. They are chauffeured around by their parents to their various organised activities, and taken on foreign holidays. If asked, they would most probably describe their childhood as 'brilliant', or as Joanna Hart does, give it their ultimate accolade and say, '*Yeah, it's really cool*'.

They are safer in some ways in their warm, comfortable world. At least they are not playing on dangerous farm machinery, sledging down on to railway lines or swimming in the river Trent with nothing but an old inner tube to keep them afloat.

But nowadays, strangers are no longer easily identifiable, and parents must be ever vigilant for their children's safety. These days, the dangers children encounter are more likely to be from over indulgence in some form or other of addictive substance. Either alcohol or prohibited drugs, pushed at them by 'dealers' and 'pushers' who lurk around school gates even in small towns like Bingham.

Childhood is a time for fun, and no one should rob a child of that magic time of life.

Happily for them, the children we interviewed from throughout the century, have mostly had wonderful childhoods. The constant theme is...*we had so much fun.*

During the course of this project, we have come to care very much for our interviewees. We value them for the insights they have given us of life in Bingham over the century, and hope that we may count them amongst our friends for many years to come.

We are proud and privileged to have been chosen by the Nottinghamshire Living History Archive Millenium Award Scheme to complete this project, and hope that it will prove of some interest to students in the years to come.

Acknowledgements

We would like to express our grateful thanks to the following people and organisations:

Alan Howe

Denis Whitaker

Peter Smith – Headteacher of Robert Miles Junior School

Phil Meakin

David Lowe

Bob Garland

Brian Middlemiss

D.P. Charlton

Chris Williams – Headteacher of Toot Hill Comprehensive School

Janet Dobson

John Broadbent

Mike Elliott

Ruth King

Rose Whittaker

Carol Haynes

The Evening Post and South Notts Advertiser

All those people interviewed on tape for this project (as listed in the Introduction)

All staff and members of the NLHA who have trained and assisted us in producing this book, (as listed in the Preface).